THE ROLE OF TOP MANAGEMENT IN THE CONTROL OF INVENTORY

George W. Plossl

W. Evert Welch

Reston Publishing Company, Inc.
A Prentice-Hall Company
Reston, Virginia

658.787
P729
c.2

Library of Congress Cataloging in Publication Data

Plossl, George W.
  The role of top management in the control of inventory.

  Bibliography: p.
  Includes index.
  1. Inventory control.   2. Industrial management.
I.   Welch, W. Evert, joint author.   II.   Title.
HD55.P53   658.7'87   78-13479
ISBN 0-8359-6697-6

© 1979 by Reston Publishing Company, Inc.
A Prentice-Hall Company
Reston, Virginia 22090

10   9   8   7   6   5   4   3   2

Printed in the United States of America

CONTENTS

The top management edict that inventory be reduced is described as a necessary element of a continuing three-pronged thrust for improved customer service, increased net earnings and reduced working assets, particularly inventory.

Inventory is portrayed as the logical and inevitable result of manufactured outputs that lag inputs of direct labor and purchased materials. Unwanted inventories are described as

Chapter 2   An Inventory Overview (cont.)

true liabilities, contrasted to the conventional assumption that they are low-grade assets. Inventory functions are identified and the benefits of modern techniques questioned.

Chapter 3   The Handles On Inventory   25

The ability of top management to come to grips with the control of inventory is pictured as a process of taking a firm grasp on four *handles* available to it.

Chapter 4   Handle #1—Fast Response To Change   33

Establishing acceptable tolerances on important variables, recognizing that they have been exceeded, and implementing effective corrective actions are considered the number one handle to aid control of inventory. *Manufacturing control* is defined as the planning and control of priorities and capacities.

Inventory problems are reduced to the bare fundamentals and explained in terms of the inputs and outputs that created the inventory. The real control possible through use of this handle is described.

This schedule, planned outputs projected in time sequence, is the instrument that generates all of the supporting activities planning. It becomes the key to resource, materials, capacity and financial planning as well as to effective budgeting, performance measurement and customer service.

The use of this handle as a means of control of manufacturing has only recently come into its own. Formerly considered a static, inflexible, operating characteristic, modern manufacturing systems now view it as a dynamic, pliable tool for priority control and a vital element in the validity of the master plan.

Chapter 11   Insist Your Organization Execute The Plan   119

Emphasis is placed on working to a sound plan, not revising it. Two alternatives are described as counterproductive: one is the development of elaborate, informal subsystems that depend completely on personalities; the other is too-frequent replanning that keeps the formal system in a constant state of flux.

Chapter 12   Pitfalls To Avoid   131

Real-life examples are used to illustrate some fundamental mistakes often made in manufacturing management. Working around the formal system, unsound management decrees, mismanagement of the master production schedule, overwhelming paper controls and naive middle-management reactions are described.

**Appendix   Planning And Controlling Priorities
And Capacities   137**

PREFACE

One of the major unanswered questions in the minds and conversations of management today is, "Where are the handles on inventory?" The writings of government economists, financial journal editors, and academicians all stress the role of inventories in business cycles, cash flow problems and return on investment but offer little or no assistance to managers on how to make inventory behave. Although it is recognized as the only really untapped source of capital, and the common company, like the common man in this country, is under-invested and over-borrowed, it is amazing how few managers know how to control inventory.

This book begins where others leave off. It acknowledges the importance of control of inventories and wastes none of the reader's time reinforcing an already over-strong case. It focuses on specific, tested, practical, universal handles by which management can bring inventories to desired levels—and then hold them there. It also offers real help in deciding how much inventory is needed, not by elegant, mysterious mathematical "models" but with straight-forward, logical methods. And it is written in business English by two men whose years of experience in diverse types of businesses are unmatched.

INTRODUCTION

In the context of this book, the term "top management" is applied to that group of individuals who have responsibility for all phases of the business. Manufacturing, Marketing, Engineering and Finance all report to them; they may have come from any of these disciplines. They may or may not have had direct operating experience and they are likely to be unfamiliar with modern techniques in Production and Inventory Control. They will be at the top management level of any company and they may also be executives at group and company levels in large companies.

What we believe these individuals should know and how we think they can function most effectively to the good of the overall company are the subjects to which this book is addressed. We can not and do not expect the same depth of technical know-how of them that we would expect of top manufacturing management. It is our hope to improve their leadership and support of Manufacturing through an improved understanding of its problems and potential.

While this book is addressed to top management, as defined, we hope it will prove useful to all levels of management, particularly those in Manufacturing who must react to top management's demands and provide information from which it can make sound judgments.

Peerless Topman who appears periodically in this book is a member of Top Management. He is very concerned about his company's ability to manage inventory and the business. Properly named "Peerless", he is a cut above most of his peers. He is fully responsible for all phases of his business; Marketing, Engineering and Finance, in addition to Manufacturing.

His flair is for management on an overall, broad-gauged basis. However, he sees inventory as both an asset, when it works for him, and a liability, when it does not, and he is determined to place its control in its rightful place in the management spectrum. It has been our privilege to work with some of the great Mr. Topmans in industry. We know they will recognize their contributions to this book.

1
TOP MANAGEMENT PRESSURE IS A MUST!

The Primary Goals

The most important near-term controllable objectives of any business are:

- net earnings
- customer service and sales
- working assets (particularly inventory)

It is obvious that there are definite interactions among these three but there are very real and commonly-held misconceptions about these interactions. For example, it is generally believed that:

- improvement in net earnings requires increased inventories
- improved customer service requires increased inventories
- reduced inventories must result in lower profits, poorer customer service or both

The three objectives, increased profits, improved customer service and reduced inventories are customarily described as being in *conflict* with each other, and top management is pictured in the role of a referee, making necessary but unhappy choices between alternatives presented by

1

Sales, Manufacturing and Financial executives in their own selfish interests. Likewise, conflict among these executives is viewed as inevitable and normal.

Let us dispel these misconceptions at the outset. *Top management's*

Peerless
Topman
Says . . .

"Keep constant and unrelenting pressure on all three goals; higher net earnings, better customer service and lower inventories."

true role is keeping constant and unrelenting pressure on all three goals. These three goals are not always in conflict. Top management's decisions can be much more constructive than making undesirable compromises between desirable alternatives. This is a book on *improving* inventory management. It will focus directly on the *handles* available to management to accomplish desired results with *better* inventories that too many believe are achievable only with *larger* inventories.

At All Costs, Avoid the INSANE Cycle

It is generally recognized that panic programs are a sure sign of mismanagement. More dangerous than any other mistake management can make is falling into the trap of focusing on one goal at a time to increase effectiveness through concentrated attention. Many managers believe this to be good management by objectives; nothing could be further from the truth.

A classic mistake made by too many managers is to shift direction periodically, now attacking excess inventory, next improving customer service and then instituting profit improvement activities, only to find inventories again out of control. In his book, *Manufacturing Control: The*

Last Frontier for Profits, George W. Plossl called this the INSANE cycle to highlight the futility of such shifts in emphasis from INventory to SAles to Net Earnings. These cycles characteristically vary in length from a few months to a year. It's amazing how many companies are following this approach and are in the same phase of the cycle at the same time, all concentrating on slashing inventories, next rebuilding sales and then restoring profit margins. The effect on the business cycle is obvious.

The more effective any one phase is and the more quickly it is accomplished, the more certain it will be to destroy whatever good came out of the previous phase and all the more certain it is to make the following phase more necessary and difficult. *Like an animal in quicksand, struggling harder simply hastens doom.* The secret of success is continual and unrelenting pressure on all three goals, not fragmented, self-perpetuating assaults on any one.

What Comes First?

A famous songwriter was once asked, "When you write a song that becomes a big hit, which comes first, the words or the music?" To everyone's surprise, his answer was, "Neither! What comes first is the telephone call!" He went on to explain that every really big number he had written had been the result of a telephone call from some producer or music publisher who needed a song for a particular show or occasion.

In one large corporation's monthly management meeting, a detailed explanation was always required for significant inventory changes and trends in each of several subsidiaries. Invariably the explanation for a company's inventory increases was that sales were increasing, requiring additional inventory. Just as invariably, other companies would explain that inventory increases had resulted from unexpected sales decreases. One top executive, deeply involved in inventory improvement programs, finally reacted with the caustic remark, "Inventory goes up because sales are up! Inventory goes up because sales are down! When in hell does inventory ever go down?" He, better than anyone else in the room, knew the answer to his own question. Inventory goes down when top management says that it must! And, it stays down only as long as top management sustains the pressure. Nothing happens until top management makes such pressure real. *The edict is a must!* It is more important than better systems, more accurate forecasts, sophisticated mathematical techniques and elegant computer programs which many so-called experts tout as vital to success.

Above all, top management must be fearless in support of its edicts. Inventory control has long been the plaything of advocates of Operations Research and Management Science who picture it with the mumbo jumbo of complex ordering models, linear programming and queuing theory, all preceded by statistical forecasting. The use of these well-intended, but often misapplied, techniques is supposed to result in achieving magical, "optimum" levels of inventory. A strong case is made that "less than optimum" is likely to be even more harmful than "more than optimum."

There is little reason to fear the consequences of insufficient inven-

Peerless Topman Says . . .

"The top-management edict is a must. Inventory goes down only when top management says it must."

tory resulting from a well-managed inventory improvement program. If asked to set a prudent objective for such a program we recommend a seven-to-ten percent reduction each year for at least five years. Several companies have been successful in such efforts. It can be done. If this objective sounds unambitious, consider what would be needed to raise this much new capital. Add the actions required to achieve the accompanying benefits of improved productivity plus other potential gains from well-managed inventory improvement programs and the value of such programs is clear.

Nothing is as certain to lead to failure of inventory improvement programs as top management complacency. Commendations, such as, "Well done!!" or "You did a great job!" when an inventory reduction goal is met may be appropriate but must never be construed as ending the program or relieving the pressure to do even better. Today's best must become tomorrow's standard. *Inventory levels never stand still; if they aren't subjected to continuous reduction efforts, they will increase.* Many companies have gone through three cycles of inventory reduction, management complacency and unnecessary increase in inventory in a ten-year period. Complacency and control are opposites.

Top Management Cannot Avoid Direct Involvement

Particularly in a large company, it may be tempting to top management to give middle management the assignment of reducing inventory without adversely affecting earnings or customer service without themselves becoming involved in the details of how it is to be done. This is usually unsuccessful.

It really should be no surprise. It is impractical to think that the various divisions of a business will magically submerge their particular interests and begin suddenly to think only of the good of the whole. A Sales department always has been and always will be most interested in serving the customer. It thinks of inventory only as necessary for supporting sales and it can be expected to resist inventory decreases. Manufacturing is measured on its ability to control the major costs of running the business. In its view, reduced costs require running larger production batches and more level, stable output rates which mean increases in inventory. Engineering is concerned with product development and improvement and feels no responsibility for any resulting material obsolescence. Finance shares top management's concern for sound asset management but has no real control of the functions of the business which affect inventory. Only top management can develop a consensus among such divergent views.

All effective inventory improvement programs start with a series of events leading up to accepted, realizable budgets for the coming fiscal year. These events, to be discussed in detail later, begin with top management setting specific objectives for operating management, followed by a series of negotiations culminating in the agreed-upon budgets, including the proposed improvements. Control is achieved through monthly progress reports to top management with in-depth explanations of unexpected problems and significant deviations. Top management cannot escape its role in setting the goals, participating in the negotiations and conducting the progress reviews. Nothing else works.

Improvement Programs Must Be Continuous

If inventory is to be kept under control, top management has no alternative but to keep continuous pressure on it. Inventory at every level and in every form must be the subject of continual, active improvement programs. Middle management must learn to accept the fact that inventory ranks with sales, net earnings and new product development in the need for continual attention. It is too important to the success of a business to be relegated to sporadic bursts of reduction efforts, half-hearted and self-defeating drives to meet "the boss's latest edict" and token attention to inventory control because "that's someone else's problem, not mine." *Its importance makes anything short of constant, unremitting pressure, directed by top management and involving all of middle management, too little too late.*

Peerless Topman Says . . .

"Set inventory goals, participate in all negotiated compromises, and review programs frequently."

Some managers believe inventory management is a very complex job, requiring complex systems on large computers using sophisticated mathematical formulas. They think the job's hopeless until they get these tools. Strangely enough, those with such systems frequently find the job harder than before. Many executives now recognize that it takes an edict, such as, "Get one million out of inventory by the end of the year." This works. Handled properly it will be more effective than any other approach. The edict is only the beginning, however. Be careful how you set the reduction target and don't dictate too short a time in which to reach it. Begin with a carefully derived edict, but don't stop there!

2

AN INVENTORY OVERVIEW

Why Inventory Behaves As It Does

Inventory is a peculiar sort of a beast that almost never seems to act according to theory nor does it respond to changes in operating activities the way one might expect. To many, it seems to be subject to the whims and fancies of some capricious god entirely unsympathetic to management's goals. On the other hand, it responds readily to specific management pressures. Good control of inventory requires a clear understanding of why it is needed, how it functions and why it seeks *natural* levels that always seem to be somewhat higher than those which now exist and a lot higher than are preferred.

When a company or a new product is in its startup phase, management pours material, labor and burden into the business and nothing comes out for a while. Later, labor and material are combined to produce a saleable product and the business realizes some output but, for a long time, this output is less than the input. The difference between input and output stays in the business and is called inventory. It continues to grow until the output eventually equals the input; then total inventory stabilizes.

From this time forward, increases in inventory can result from both what is done and what is not done within the business. *Practically every management error shows up in excess inventory.* Unexpected errors in forecasts, poorly-timed product design changes, inept purchasing practices, manufacturing problems and other mistakes in the management of the business all add to inventory by increasing input or lowering output.

Inventory stabilizes only when outputs equal inputs. This is the only certainty. The complexity of the activities affecting it are such that actual

Peerless
Topman
Says . . .

"To control inventory, balance total outputs—shipments—against total inputs— purchased material or productive labor."

inventory levels are seldom close to planned levels; control of inventories rarely achieves the same success as other capital investments. You can estimate the cost and construction schedule of a building, you can invest in a machine tool expecting certain benefits and you can draw the line on receivables by limiting credit, all with a good chance of meeting plan. It seems to be self-regulating. It isn't, of course, and will readily respond to pressures to reduce it but such reductions must be carefully planned, prudent and reasonable. Attempts at drastic and sudden improvements inevitably fail. It takes a delicate touch. Overpower the situation, shut off inputs too suddenly and the outputs will simply drop, if you're lucky, only enough to match the fall-off in input.

Inventory—Asset or Liability?

The farmer's inventory is in heads of cattle, hogs or sheep, bushels of grain or standing timber. These determine his prosperity and measure his net worth. The local hardware store's inventory is a wide variety of goods on the shelves and counters, attractive and useful to customers and available for immediate delivery. The housewife's inventory is packaged and canned goods on the shelves and fresh and frozen foods in the refrigerator-freezer;

their presence in the house provides materials for a choice of meals without daily visits to the market. All these inventories have clearly visible, tangible benefits to their owners.

In manufacturing, inventory is always counted as an asset on financial balance sheets. It is an important factor in the acquisition or sale of a going business. It is a significant portion, frequently the major share, of the total assets of any company. It is truly an asset, however, only to the extent that its existence is justified by some tangible benefit or return. *Inventory is truly an asset when its makeup is appropriate to the business at hand and the total is in accordance with the plan.* Such an investment in inventory pays its way and earns an adequate return in addition to making the sales outputs possible. Those portions of inventory in excess of need and above planned totals represent investments which have become liabilities. The goal of top management must be reduction of these portions of total inventory, the elimination of investments that fail to pay their way and become an unnecessary burden to the business.

Although financial statements call it an asset, most top managers view and treat inventory as a liability. "We've always got too much." "Our turnover is too low." Such comments clearly reveal this. The Sales Manager, concerned with poor deliveries and new markets, sees the need

Peerless Topman Says . . .

"*Inventory is an asset. Identify a specific, tangible, adequate return on the investment; it is a liability when no such return can be identified.*"

for, and the value of, more. Manufacturing managers fear downtime and want stable, level production, requiring more inventory. Top management and the Controller, however, see inventory as funds tied up, unavailable for other uses. Their main concern is with other needs for capital, cash flow, transfers among classes of inventory and *reserves* against the contingency (usually a certainty) that some inventory eventually will be found to be valueless.

Recognizing which inventories are indeed assets and could well be increased, and which are liabilities and should be reduced, is an important responsibility of management. Unfortunately, today's accounting systems are not geared to this type of thinking: improvements to make this possible are badly needed. No financial reporting system has ever been set up to identify graduations in inventory value from full current cost down to zero and, even in some real instances, below zero. Recognition that a considerable portion of inventory is actually in excess of current need is common. This is a true liability. But, identifying and putting a specific value on such inventory is difficult, although necessary, in developing successful programs to reduce inventory and also in operating systems successfully to avoid their inadvertant replacement. Inventory is the most revealing indicator of the quality of a management team. The opportunity to improve is tremendous in most companies. Capturing the benefits of increased returns on reduced investments requires clear distinctions between inventory as a liability and as an asset. This involves understanding the functions of inventory and how it earns some tangible return.

How Inventory Becomes a Liability

Order-quantities too large at the time they are produced generate large liabilities in inventory. Even more prevalent are unwanted inventories that result from poor schedules that bring in unneeded materials. Lead times are usually set without consideration of the resultant inventory and then poorly managed; any resemblance between actual and planned lead times is too often coincidental. However, the vast majority of excesses are the result of changing conditions, new requirements or unforeseen problems that make the original plan for inputs and outputs inappropriate or unattainable.

Let's look at a few examples. Because of a purchase discount, 100 pieces of an item are brought in to meet expected requirements over five weeks of 20 pieces each week. The inventory will be 80 at the end of the first week and will drop to zero at the end of the fifth if things go according to plan. The inventory is truly an asset. The return on the investment comes from lower purchase price and ordering costs. Should the requirement for 20 per week disappear after the first week because of a design change, the inventory of 80 is now excess and a continuing liability until it is finally worked off. If the first requirement of 20 to be met by the order for 100 is needed at the start of week 10 but the order arrives in week 6, there is an excess inventory—a liability—of 100 for four weeks. The liability becomes an asset again at the start of week 10, unless requirements decrease or are postponed. If the early receipt was planned in anticipation of possible earlier demand, the inventory, now called *safety stock,* is properly considered to be an asset.

If manufacturing requires six weeks from starting an order for 100 pieces to process it to completion, there is an *in process* inventory of 100 during that time. If the total amount of work-in-process for all open orders is enough to avoid interruptions in production from lack of materials, the inventory is properly considered an asset. The return comes from avoiding the expense of downtime or paying the premium cost of subcon-

Peerless Topman Says . . .

"Look for liability inventory when plans are changed significantly and when management makes errors of judgment."

tracting the work to someone else. If, on the other hand, the inventory is there four weeks too long because of inept planning or control of priorities and capacity, then it must be considered as an inadvertent liability for that time.

The Fallacy of Depending Upon Techniques

There is a widely-held impression that inventories are created by three pieces of information on a purchase or production order: the identifying name and number of the item; the quantity or batch size to be run, and the due date for delivery of material into inventory. When the order quantity exceeds immediate requirements, it is assumed that it creates a *working* inventory which will average about half of the order size. Obviously, the larger the order quantity, the larger the inventory. If the new order calls for delivery before the remainder of the previous lot has been used, a *planned safety stock* will result equal to the stock on hand at the time the new order arrives. The order quantity and the length of time it is being worked on (the manufacturing lead time) will determine the resultant work-in-process inventory.

The implications seem clear; inventory will be generated by the techniques used to answer the multitude of "How much?" and "When?" questions that arise each day. Using rigorous ordering techniques, it is possible to calculate the inventories that will result *if the plan is executed.* Refinements to those techniques should result in predictable changes in inventory. The theory of these "How much?" and "When?" decisions and the proper *techniques* to apply this theory have been investigated by countless practitioners, consultants and teachers resulting in thousands of pages of writing on inventory control. Formulas for order quantities and safety stocks have run the full gamut from the crudest of rules to the most sophisticated of mathematical models. Most of our so-called "advanced" inventory control techniques involve the use of some mathematical formula or *model.* The theory on which these various formulas are based is sound; each has some limitations, however. Lack of recognition of these limitations is responsible for the formula's frequent failures. The Economic Order Quantity (EOQ) formula has been in constant use since 1915, yet failure to understand one single, simple limitation is responsible for millions of dollars of excess inventory in many companies today.

The formula simply does not recognize that the total of all future requirements may be less than the calculated order quantity. The formula uses "future usage" (in average weekly, monthly or annual quantities), assuming that this will go on indefinitely and that the quantity ordered will be used entirely. To see how far astray a good technique can go, look at some items in inventory classed as "slow moving," determine the current monthly usage and compare it to the figure used when the last order quantity calculation was made and the last order released. Months of supply in calculated order quantities rarely exceed 12; months of supply of inventories on hand often exceed 100.

Too many people try to fit one technique to a wide variety of situations for simplicity of application. For example, an item needed in quantities of 600 once every six months will not be controlled well if its usage is defined as "100 per month." Some averages are useful: this one is not. This is also true of mathematical forecasting models where people attempt to match the forecast period to the planning frequency, say one week. A total of 5,200 may be an accurate forecast for the annual demand for a device, but 100 per week may be a very poor forecast.

Top management must be wary of recommendations from inside or outside "experts" that more sophisticated techniques be implemented. We have seen more harm than good come from adopting esoteric order-quantity formulas like IBM's "Part-Period Balancing with Look Ahead and Look Back," not because of inherent weaknesses in the technique or the theory upon which it rests, but because practitioners fail to think through the results of applying the techniques in the unified, dynamic environment of their systems.

Peerless Topman Says . . .

"Beware of sophisticated techniques; better work is done with simple tools in skilled hands."

Every technique, no matter how valid and useful, needs managing—full understanding of its terms, assumptions and limitations and fast response to changes. Proper application of theory, formulas and techniques in a sound overall system is really important, seeking technical improvements to the formulas is not.

Many practitioners have been disappointed in applying popular techniques. Shop loading has been around for a long time, having been possible since work measurement techniques were first introduced about 1900. It never accomplished the job of capacity planning and control which everyone applied it to, causing continuous over-correction and imbalance. In the late 1960s professionals in the field recognized that "load," the amount of work *in* a work center *at a point in time*, is not "capacity," which is the amount of work going *through* a work center *during some period of time*. Machine or shop loading is a priority control tool, measuring the ability of a work center to stay on schedule, not a capacity planning or control technique at all.

In the 1960s the availability of computers and data collection terminals tempted many managers to develop *shop floor control systems,* tracking in detail the location and progress of every manufacturing lot on the plant floor. This was certainly the place to see all the problems—lost orders, skipped operations, poor counts, unreported scrap, etc.—and the lure of increased labor productivity justified large expenditures for *systems* to get better control. Unfortunately, attacking the symptoms didn't help cure the real diseases—too many open orders and poor priority information. As one manager who had invested more than $150,000 in such a system told George Plossl, "Now I can get all the wrong orders finished on time."

Even Material Requirements Planning, which swept the country in the late '60s and early '70s because of the soundness of its concepts, has little value as a stand-alone technique. It depends upon Capacity Requirements Planning, Input/Output Control, Scheduling, Loading and Priority Control functions to support it and, above all, on accurate data it can use and on an achievable Master Production Schedule to drive it. Far too little time has been devoted to studies of this technique; master scheduling had received practically no attention prior to 1970.

It is an enlightening and sobering exercise to take a real inventory in a warehouse or stockroom, use the ordering rules supposedly applied, calculate the model or *standard* inventory and compare it to what is actually on hand. Rarely is the actual less than twice the standard. Expand the exercise to include work-in-process and the difference will be even more surprising. The theory and its application are widely different. Approached one item at a time, control of inventories never achieves the promises of the theory.

Excessive inventories are more often the result of ineffective management rather than ineptly-calculated order quantities and safety stocks. We said earlier that all of the mistakes of management find their way into inventory. Record errors hide excesses and the failure to anticipate that an expensive part will be eliminated by an engineering change shortly after the receipt of a substantial replenishment batch results in obsolete inventory. Both are beyond the control of theory and ordering rules.

In a depression many years ago, a company with whom Evert Welch was working became ultraconservative. The manufacturing plan was set to produce at a constant rate only those products which were saleable beyond any shadow of a doubt. Without any changes in order quantity or safety stock rules, the inventory-to-sales ratio dropped about 40 percent to a level never achieved before or in many later years of normal operation. Later studies led to the conclusion that the key was the ratio of actual shipments in a given month to those predicted for that month four months earlier. The higher this ratio, the lower the inventory. Making a good plan four months out, and then hitting it, made the difference. They concentrated on improving the forecast of total future demand and then reacted quickly and effectively to change output rates as demand changed rather than concentrating on refinements of the individual item *techniques* which they had previously thought controlled inventory. Effective inventory control will result only through combining the proper techniques in a unified manufacturing control system. Much like a chain with unequal strength links, there is no advantage in improving an adequate individual technique when another system element is lacking or is ineffective.

Inventory Classified by Function

We have mentioned the need for accounting systems which distinguish between inventories that are truly assets and those that are liabilities. Even before that, steps should be taken to get away from complete dependence on the conventional raw material/work-in-process/finished goods

Peerless Topman Says . . .

"Identify the functions of inventory by which it earns a tangible return on the investment: accounting classes hide these."

categories now found in all accounting reports. Inventories exist to support certain functions and are thus capable of earning a return on the required investment. For those deeply involved, the subject is discussed in detail in George W. Plossl's *Manufacturing Control: The Last Frontier for Profits* (Reston, VA: Reston Publishing Company, Inc., 1973). Top management should at least understand the five functions and the category of inventory associated with each.

Lot-Size Inventories

Many inventories exist because it is economical to manufacture or purchase materials in batches that are larger than immediate need. These can be found in all the accounting classes—raw materials, stocked purchased and manufactured parts, work-in-process and finished goods inventories.

The savings come from reducing the number of orders and process equipment setups to be made. The function of such inventories is to decouple manufacturing operations so that they can be operated most economically. Lot-sizing techniques make it possible to draw trade-off curves, such as that in Figure 2-1, relating specific amounts of such inventory with definite returns. Management is thus freed from determining some magic cost-of-carrying inventory and can make decisions on increasing or decreasing the investment in this category on the basis of whether or not the capital could earn a better return if utilized elsewhere.

Figure 2-1   Trade-Off Curve

Interestingly enough, average work-in-process inventories are not affected by lot-sizing. In a year, 12 months' worth of an item has to be processed over a normal lead time, creating inventory during this period. Whether the work is done in one lump or divided into several lots does not affect the average. Note what this really means: Work-in-process will be directly proportional to lead time. The benefits from reducing manufacturing cycle times can be easily calculated. Since no real costs are incurred until output actually suffers, this should be receiving maximum management attention instead of being almost completely ignored.

Demand-Fluctuation Inventories

The theory and techniques applicable to this inventory, generally called *safety stock,* are discussed in detail in the Appendix. This inventory is intended to absorb fluctuations in demand during the replenishment period that cannot or are not planned to be handled through replanning, rescheduling or other corrective actions. Its function is to protect customer service, making extra material available in case of need. Using the theory, trade-off curves (Figure 2-2) showing the additional inventory required to provide improved service levels can be drawn. In this way, management can study alternatives rather than guessing at the "right service level" with no knowledge of the investment needed to achieve it.

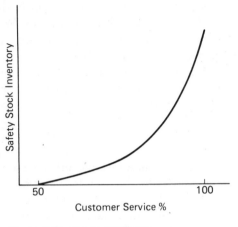

Figure 2-2   Trade-Off Curve

Supply-Fluctuation Inventories

These are inventories planned to accommodate the uncertainty of vendor performance. Their function is the same as safety stock; in this case the *customer* is your plant and you are planning *insurance* against purchased material shortages. Decisions are handled the same as with demand-fluctuation inventories.

Anticipation Inventory

Anticipation inventory most often occurs as finished goods intended to permit operating at a level manufacturing rate over some period. This is desirable to meet seasonal demand, to carry over a plant vacation shutdown or to continue operation during a plant move or major rearrangement. Its function is to reduce the need for changes in capacity. The payback comes from savings when people do not have to be hired, laid off or retrained, and from reduced scrap, rework and similar wastes when capacity changes are avoided. The alternatives can be studied using the PSI report discussed in Chapter 5.

In-Process and Transportation Inventories

Inventory in the manufacturing process and inventory being transported from one place to another are both dependent upon the magnitude of the flow and the time flowing. In each case, the flow rate is dependent on the level of business activity. Lead time or transit time, therefore, becomes the factor which determines the amount of inventory; slow down the flow and inventory will increase and vice versa. The function of such inventories is to keep the pipeline full. They earn a return if the costs (freight and material handling) of moving inventory can be reduced. Higher speed costs more money; the savings with slower movement of in-transit materials may be an adequate return on the added investment.

Hedge Inventories

Anticipated strikes, price increases and other reasons an item may be in short supply invite a user to "buy while the price is right" or "get some while they're available," leading to an accumulation of inventory in advance. The line between reasonable hedging and outright speculation can be a pretty fine one at times. While it can be extremely profitable, speculation had best be left to the specialists since it is an entirely different business from manufacturing. The return on investment implications and the function of hedge inventories are obvious.

Analyzing the Make-Up of an Inventory

In preparing summary reports of existing inventories by function, hedge inventories are fairly easy to identify as are anticipation inventories. Data on present work-in-process inventories are the only ones found in standard accounting reports. Total planned lot-size inventory can only be determined by adding up individual item order quantities. The same approach will give total planned safety stock. Actual lot-size and safety stock inventories can be determined by deducting all other classes from the total.

Measurements of Inventory

Much has been written on ways to measure inventory. Most of this literature attempts to evaluate total inventory resulting from the use of various ordering rules. Later in this chapter we will address the question, "How much inventory is enough?" and the importance of setting valid budgets. Now, however, we are concerned with determining whether, in fact, an inventory actually increased or decreased significantly. Changes in the gross dollar totals can be very misleading without considering at the same time variations in other factors of the business.

All useful inventory measures are, therefore, ratios in which inventory is related to some other activity such as sales, shipments or production output. In a maintenance supply stockroom or a raw material stores, the dollar value of the inventory may be related to the annual output of materials from the stores in comparable dollars and a ratio or a percentage calculated. A decrease from 20 percent to 16 percent measures a valid reduction in inventory irrespective of changes up or down in the total rate of output.

The proper determination of *annualized output* is a matter of judgment rather than rigorous calculations. We always recommend some simple, consistent approach which is easily understood and applied. There is a wide variety of choices. The preceding year's actual data could be used, the preceding half-year times two, the preceding quarter times four or the preceding month times 12. Forecasts are more difficult but more meaningful to use. The projection of output next month times 12, the coming quarter forecast times four, the coming half-year times two or the forecast for next year might be used. Annualizing year-to-date output or using a fixed forecast for the current calendar year are also possibilities. It is not mandatory that both inventory and output data be in comparable dollars. Many companies use ratios of inventory in *cost* dollars and output in *sales* dollars. Consistency is important, of course.

One of the most effective reporting systems we have seen in multidivisional corporations relates current inventories at cost to year-to-date sales annualized. Apples and oranges? Of course! Ineffective? Not at all! The managers of the many companies involved have been using this measure for years. Like any measurements, the conclusions reached by using them are always subject to interpretation; managers must understand the measures and recognize their limitations.

Some valid objections can be raised to the use of every one of these alternatives. The accounting professionals are debating *inflation costing* as well as the older standard, average and actual costs and LIFO or FIFO, all of which affect the valuation of inventory. Unfortunately, operating managers cannot wait until the best approach is found (we doubt it ever will be). They must get control now. Their principal need is a series of consecutive, practical calculations to show whether the trend of inventory is up or down. The absolute value of the inventory is of secondary importance. Using the same indicator period after period, year after year, a manager can react promptly and correctly to significant change.

Ratios can be calculated two ways. Inventory divided by output is usually called *percentage of inventory to output,* or *cents of inventory per dollar of output.* Dividing output by inventory gives the more commonly used *turnover.* Whether $150,000 of inventory with output of $600,000 is called 25 percent *inventory to output* or *turnover* of four is obviously a matter of individual preference. Some industries seem to favor one over the other and some managers like to compare their operations to competitors and others in similar businesses and would choose accordingly.

One of the greatest exercises in futility is comparison of one company's inventory ratios to that of another, supposedly "similar," company.

Peerless Topman Says . . .

"Use simple, practical measures of inventory performance. Watch them constantly and react quickly to adverse trends."

Nevertheless, the publication of annual statements triggers many an analysis of comparable inventory ratios. Whereas finding out that a competitor has 18 percent ratio of year-end inventory to sales last year while yours was 21 percent may be interesting, it is not likely to tell you whose business is the better managed. There are too many possible but hidden differences—in customer service and employment policies, in value added, manufacturing technologies and distribution practices, to name a few. Dun and Bradstreet publishes an annual report of ranges of inventory ratios for many groups of manufacturing firms. The range for every product grouping is so broad that it precludes any reasonable conclusion about what is good or bad. It's like comparing your golf scores with those of other duffers in your club; you can feel pretty good if no one brings up the subject of par. To make inventory ratios useful, choose one that suits you, be consistent in its application and watch the deviations and trends. Don't try to establish comparability between different operations until you've given much more attention to setting par. This subject is covered in Chapter 8.

A-B-C

One of management's oldest and soundest techniques, the concept of the *vital few* and the *trivial many,* goes back to Vilfredo Pareto (about 1530) and is applied to all management areas. "This is an *A* problem," has become common language identifying a problem of major importance. "This is a *C* problem," is equally common in shrugging off something not now worthy of attention. "Why don't you do an *A-B-C?*" is widely recognized as suggesting ranking a group of problems in descending order of importance.

Peerless Topman Says . . .

"Make the most of one of management's oldest and most effective techniques, A-B-C, the ranking of problems in descending sequence from the most important to the least."

One bright young executive takes his incoming mail the first thing each business day and "does an *A-B-C.*" The two or three most important letters are his *A* items and he handles them personally. The top half of the rest is his *B* list and his supervisors handle them. The remaining *C* list is turned over to clerks for routine handling.

The most common *A-B-C* list of all is found in inventory control where a group of similar items, such as those in a given stockroom, are ranked in descending order of annual dollar usage. The top section of the list is *A*, the bottom is the *C* with the *B*'s in between. Divisions between them are arbitrary and changeable. A cumulative total of the dollar usages will always demonstrate very high concentration of total dollar usage at the top of the list. Typically in manufacturing, the first five percent of the items will include 50 percent of the total activity. The list tends to be symmetrical, with the last 50 percent of the items involving only five percent of the usage. Distribution and retail inventories tend to have flatter curves with more uniform distribution of the items. At the top, or A end of the list, significant reductions in inventory can be realized by keeping order quantities (in terms of time supply) low. At the bottom or C end, real savings in order handling can be achieved by increasing order quantities and reducing the frequency of orders.

In addition to ranking by dollar activity, other rankings are useful. These include unit cost (what items will be most subject to theft and should have really accurate records?); unit volume (what items will require the most cubage in storage?); dollar inventory (where are the real reduction potentials?) and shelf life (are we watching for potential spoilage?). There isn't any such thing as the right percentage of items in the A list and there aren't any hard and fast rules regarding how a list shall be used. It's a tool to focus attention.

Inventory and the Health of Your Business

There is a strong parallel between rising inventories and increasing weight as indicators of the health of businesses and individuals. Both are measures to be watched carefully and continuously. With both inventory and weight, an unexpected increase is a warning of potentially serious problems. It should trigger an immediate analysis of the cause and a positive program to arrest the change and return to normal. Immediate identification of the cause may be difficult, but it is vital that the problems be identified and stabilized as fast as possible before conditions get too far out of control. Businesses, like people and their weight, have different *natural levels* of inventory, so size alone is not a good danger signal. Likewise, stable levels of weight and inventory are no proof of good health. Most businesses have excess inventories just as most people are overweight, even though stability exists. Most people and most businesses are conscious of the need to reduce and go through periodic reduction programs; few work at it seriously and continuously. Those who do, however, get a payback that far exceeds the efforts involved. The lean are healthier, happier and live longer than the obese.

The most successful inventory reduction programs result from properly identifying inputs (i.e., batch quantities, early receipts) that can be decreased without affecting outputs and finding outputs that can be increased without increasing inputs (i.e., reducing back orders). Pinpointing such inputs and outputs can be a challenging job, like identifying the proper dietary change for weight reduction. Cutting out only bread and potatoes works well for some people and simply reducing planned safety stocks will benefit some businesses. Other people may have to work harder and suffer more, doing without sweets, alcohol and other goodies and

Peerless Topman Says . . .

"Watch your inventory as you watch your weight. A sudden or unexpected change in either is a sign of potential serious trouble."

other businesses may find it necessary to buckle down to the hard work of solving manufacturing problems and really meeting the final assembly schedules.

In difficult cases, and to insure that no lasting harm is done, professional guidance is recommended. The trained inventory expert knows all the possible areas of improvement, as does the family physician who is familiar with a variety of diets. However, neither the doctor nor the inventory professional can accomplish anything by simply being available. Nothing will happen until top management says, "The upward trend of inventory is wrong and must be arrested now. Determine the causes and implement corrective steps immediately to eliminate excess inventories. Then let me know how much lower you will drop inventories in the next year. I will not be satisfied with your performance until this program is laid out and working."

3

THE HANDLES ON INVENTORY

Controlling Inventory Is Always Difficult

Every manufacturing operation of any size has thousands of items of control, and its inventory is determined by hundreds of daily decisions made by dozens of people. With modern systems, thousands of mechanized "decisions" are made by computers which print out reams of paper suggesting order releases and reschedules too numerous to handle and poorly understood by the people supposed to act on them. It is not surprising that many managers come to erroneous conclusions about inventory control. Some think real control is impossible: there are too many variables, too much uncertainty and the best hope is just to minimize chaos and troubles. Others believe control requires "peopleless," sophisticated, mechanized systems replete with elegant mathematical formulas processed on large computers. Still others pin their hopes on well-publicized but vaguely understood techniques such as MRP systems.

Controlling inventory is also difficult because it requires both a sound plan and effective, timely execution of the plan. Actions taken must consider the inescapable interactions among components of inventory and in manufacturing operations. For example, reducing order quantities and delaying planned deliveries are the first phases of most inventory reduction programs. What should be obvious, but apparently is not, is that inventory will not come down if shortages cause stalled production and pileups of almost-finished products which can't be shipped. Throttling the release of new orders to reduce work-in-process inventory is tempting but may be worse than futile if bottleneck operations sputter or stop as a result of inadequate work flow. Shortening manufacturing cycle times should cut work-in-process proportionately but lack of capacity controls may simply transfer the excess into stocked component inventories of higher value.

Peerless Topman Says . . .

"Don't let the difficulty be the excuse for lack of control of inventory. It's not easy but it can be done if you insist on it."

Improving control is never easy but it is possible. Enough companies are now hitting inventory budgets regularly to make this a statement of fact, not a pious hope. Control requires that each level of management understand where its "handles" on inventory are, how to grasp and move them and when. The average inventory control manager believes the handles are in the theory. Use the right technique on each item for determining order quantities and safety stocks, get MRP running on a computer, develop machine loads in all work centers, apply Critical Ratio to set priorities on orders in the plant, and the total will come out right. Why doesn't it? Many companies have these techniques working but they're not reducing inventories. Some others are doing a fine job of managing the total inventory investment even without these tools.

Technically sound systems are necessary but they are not sufficient for effective control of manufacturing. Formal records must be set up and maintained to show unshipped customer orders, master production schedule details, bills of material, product specifications, open-purchased and manufacturing orders, process information, time and cost standards and the myriad of other basic data needed to design, manufacture and market products. Formal procedures and associated transaction documents must be set up to enter new information into these files and to update the data already there. Notices, charts and other output reports are needed so that people may be helped to make the right decisions on time. Routine decision rules may even be built into the formal system to eliminate monotonous, repetitive work. All of these things constitute the formal system. The primary role of this system is to provide the information people need to make their daily decisions and to take the proper actions, not to make the decisions for them. It's only supposed to help managers, not replace them.

Top managements' attitude toward inventory control could best be described as "frustration." Too often they have been brainwashed to believe that inventory is some sort of special asset, the increases and decreases of which are the result of unpredictable and unmanageable influences. They have learned that inventory must grow when the business grows and have seen middle management defend that phenomenon to the death. Middle management's logical and, to them, irrefutable conclusion is that an inventory increase is a necessary preface to any sales increase. They think it's necessary to put more in before more can come out. Top management has also learned, painfully, that inventory grows sharply when a downturn comes—until the flood of incoming material and the rate of labor input are brought under control. Such movements are held to be inevitable and of unpredictable magnitude; it is also averred that supporting explanations should be unnecessary. Even the suitability of an existing level is usually justified only on the basis of historical performance, occasionally supported by comparison with so-called "similar" companies or published industry averages. Small wonder many top managers ask, "When does inventory ever go down?"

Management's Handles on Inventory

In the end, nothing seems to reduce inventory except an arbitrary top management edict compelling middle management to recognize that controlling inventory must rank high among the priorities of day-to-day management problems. All of this supports our belief that few managers at any level recognize the handles on inventory available to them, nor do many have their hands on these controls and know when to push them.

There are four major handles with which managers can make inventory behave:

1. Fast Response to Change

2. Input/Output Controls

3. The Master Production Schedule

4. Properly Managed Lead Times

Each of these will be discussed more fully in subsequent chapters. A brief introduction is needed, however, to put the idea of handles and their functions in perspective.

In the authors' early days as inventory managers, both began with an understanding of the techniques, which dealt with one item at a time. We thought that doing the "right thing"—ordering the *right amount* of the *right item* at the *right time*—would make the totals come out *right*. Like a builder without a good architectural plan, we carefully put together, piece by piece, a monstrosity.

Peerless Topman Says . . .

"Find and firmly grasp the four handles on inventory. Start with control of the totals and then the details will work out right."

It's now clear that control can be achieved only by beginning with a sound overall plan for the *totals* and then forcing the details to fit. Two of our major handles are totals which top management must develop and monitor.

Handles are also levers by which management can exert pressure on daily activities to move them in the right direction. Like all controls, however, caution must be exercised to avoid over-controlling, using too heavy a hand. Complex machines like jet aircraft and manufacturing companies need a firm, steady hand at the controls, prompt reaction to course deviations and a crew thoroughly familiar with the instruments.

Fast Response to Change—Handle No. 1

The requirements to make this effective are explained in Chapter 4. A manufacturing control system is nothing more or less than a means for identifying corrective actions needed today through a comparison of planned activities and the actions actually being taken. Emphasis should be put on taking corrective action rather than revising the program to bring plan and actual together in the near future. Time is of the essence. A vital requirement for success is prompt identification of significant changes and seeing that they are implemented. Since the number of problems identified is usually so large that all can never be handled and solved, selectivity to sort out what is important from what is not becomes a vital requirement in an effective control system. Manufacturing people customarily wait too long to act and then over-correct.

Input/Output Controls—Handle No. 2

This will be discussed in depth in Chapter 5. As was stated earlier, inventory is the net result of many inputs and outputs. When inputs exceed outputs, the inevitable result is an inventory increase: conversely, inventory decreases only when outputs exceed inputs. Input/output controls and actions can be generated for a multi-division corporation, a single company, an individual plant, a department, one work center or a machine. All levels of management must be thoroughly familiar with the two variables influencing inventory: inputs and outputs. Inventory reduction programs require decreasing inputs without reducing outputs or increasing outputs without adding to inputs. Every inventory improvement program is an effort to identify and correct errant input and output practices. Every management question about inventory size or change is answerable in terms of what happened to some specific input or output. The identification of these critical activities is an important aspect of effective inventory control.

The Master Production Schedule—Handle No. 3

Chapter 6 covers this in more detail. Every input or output action is taken in relationship to some plan, no matter how that plan is generated and whether or not it is effectively constructed and managed. The effectiveness of input and output controls and, therefore, control of inventory, is directly related to the validity of the master plan. This has created a new and important activity, applying the techniques required in the development and use of a Master Production Schedule, which is now seen as the prime mover of all manufacturing, marketing and financial planning. It charts the course for each major department, compromising or reconciling their conflicting objectives and providing a measure of how well each executes its share of the master plan.

The Management of Lead Time—Handle No. 4

This will be discussed in detail in Chapter 7. No matter how a detailed production program is generated from a Master Production Schedule, a most important consideration is the individual lead time assigned to each replenishment activity. In a chain of production or procurement events, the finish date of one becomes the earliest possible start date of the next. Finish dates for a group of items to be made into an assembly must coincide if unusable, mismatched inventory is to be avoided.

Manipulation of the manufacturing lead times, once a manufacturing operation is in process, is absolutely essential to coping with change; the fact of life is that few, if any, will occur as planned. For that reason, planned lead times cannot be minimums. Since work-in-process inventory levels are directly proportional to lead time, planning long lead times would be wasteful and they cannot be maximums. So, the choice of suitable *average planned lead times* is an essential and important part of manufacturing planning.

An important aspect of lead time control is that capacity constraints usually dictate that lead times are interactive. In other words, if you shorten one, you invariably increase others. All managers see clearly the role of priority in managing lead time—the higher the priority, the shorter the lead time. Few understand the need to manage capacity to control lead times. Even fewer know the real truth about lead time and its influence on their ability to control manufacturing operations and inventories.

Important Supports for Our Handles

Important support activities for these four handles will be discussed in detail in Chapter 8. The requirements for effective control of manufacturing are now clear:

- A realistic master production schedule, supported by a complete, integrated, formal system to plan and control material priorities and capacity. Every system needs a goal and every activity must have an objective. With inventories, the goals and objectives are best expressed in a budget. Such a budget will be effective and workable only if it is acceptable to all levels of management. The inventory budget, its development and its use are important in support of our handles, particularly in generating fast response to change.

- Accurate records of the basic data used by the system: Like it or not, we must act on the basis of information reported via displays on CRTs, written reports and analyses. Any attempt to make decisions on the basis of incorrect information is obviously doomed to produce mediocre results at best. Acceptance of record errors as a way of life is neither necessary nor prudent. Accuracy improvement, a necessary support to our handles also has unprecedented payback in short-term profit improvements.

- Qualified people running the system to help control the business. This includes both the practitioners and qualified managers running the business *with the system* and not depending solely on blind, panic-stricken, unreasoned edicts.

- An organization of all these people directed toward and capable of working together to execute the plans; not antagonists fighting each other and blaming each other for the failures to bring the plans to reality.

4

HANDLE NO. 1–FAST RESPONSE TO CHANGE

The Essence of Control

Real control requires knowing where you are now, where you want to go and having the means of getting there. The essence of control of manufacturing is having a set of sound plans, recognizing promptly when operations have deviated significantly from these plans and instituting prompt corrective action to execute the plans.

You will never control what you do not measure. This cogent statement, when applied to inventories, needs more detailed explanations of:

- specifically what to measure

- how often and when

- how accurately

- other needs in addition to measurement

If you ever have rowed a boat you are familiar with the requirements for control. To reach your destination you must look over your shoulder periodically to check your heading. The strength of water currents and wind and your desire to hold a straight course determine how often you need to look and how much you zigzag or drift off course.

There are five basic elements of control:

1. A destination, budget or plan: obviously one that's realistic, achievable, sound

2. Tolerances defining "close enough," setting significance limits on deviations from the plan which need highlighting

3. A sensing mechanism for timely, accurate detection of variances between actual and the plan

4. A feedback device to relay selected variances back to a controller

5. A controller responsible for taking corrective action promptly

Peerless Topman Says . . .

"Have a set of sound plans, recognize significant deviations and institute corrective action promptly."

In the rowboat, you set the destination and decide how much tolerance you'll permit off course. Your eyes are the sensing mechanism and your mind the feedback device that advises your muscles, the controller, which oar to pull to get back on course. This is an intermittent, periodic type of control, as are practically all inventory control systems. It's good enough to take a look at intervals, see where you are and correct if necessary.

If you're flying a jet plane in heavy traffic near an airport you need continuous readings on speed, altitude, direction and deviations from course—a *real-time, on-line* control system, obviously far more expensive and requiring higher-level professional skills to operate. Few, if any, inventory and manufacturing control systems need to be real-time, on-

line. The ultimate determination will be the ability of the controller to handle and react to information fed back. Too much data too often may only cause nervous prostration, not an improvement in control. Another important factor is how well the system model represents the real manufacturing environment. Computers are highly precise; plants and their activities are not.

Controlling inventories requires controlling production and/or procurement of many items to support uncertain rates of output of many changeable products, a far more complex task than rowing a boat or even flying a jet airplane. Contrary to the opinions of most practitioners in the field, as well as those of most managers, control of these myriad variables cannot be achieved simply by ordering the right amount of each material at the right time. Quite the opposite is true. Control involves setting the right total values for sales rates, inventory levels and plant output rates and then applying the techniques properly to each material, forcing it to live within the total constraints. Don't start with the details and assume the totals will come out right; set the totals right and make the details conform.

The Three Major Functions and the System

It is now well recognized by professionals in the field that control of manufacturing involves three major functions: making a realistic master production schedule, planning and controlling work priorities and planning and controlling capacity. The necessary elements to perform these functions in any sound formal system have also been identified and are illustrated in Figure 4-1. Notice how both priority and capacity planning and control activities are interlocked. They must be performed simultaneously, using an integrated system. Unfortunately, many companies still try to work on them independently.

As shown in Figure 4-1, the master production schedule is developed from the master production plan used for overall business and resource planning. A first-cut or rough-cut capacity plan is needed to test the master production schedule for realism. It would be senseless to go through all the detailed material and capacity planning procedures only to find out that the master production schedule was invalid at the start.

The master schedule, managements' third handle, discussed in Chapter 6, drives the material requirement's planning techniques. These indicate when new orders should be released and also maintain valid priorities on released orders for both purchased and manufactured materials. In addition, they generate information on planned orders to be released in the future to support the master production schedule. These

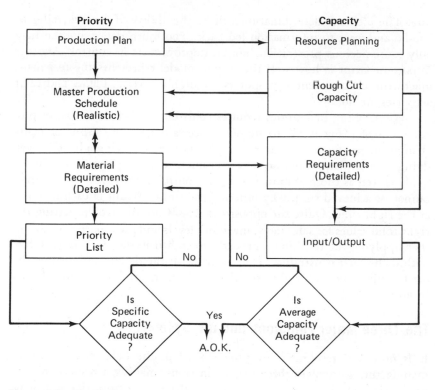

Priority   Capacity

Figure 4-1 The System

planned orders can provide information for more detailed capacity requirements planning if it is considered worthwhile. Material requirements planning feeds the priority control activities via a priority list issued periodically for each important plant work-center. Recently some companies have been providing similar priority data together with capacity information to important suppliers of purchased materials.

A vital activity missing in far too many companies is input/output capacity control, the second management handle to be covered in detail in Chapter 5. Its objective is to insure a steady flow of work at the proper rates into and out of important work centers, whether they be in your own or in a vendor's plant. This technique makes it possible to control lead times, so vital if any formal system is to function effectively. Lead time is the fourth management handle on inventory and will be covered in more detail in Chapter 7.

It is very human and sometimes valid to equate elegance and sophistication with improved capabilities. This is definitely not true, however, of manufacturing control systems; in fact, as will be explained in the Appendix, the pseudo-sophistication of many popular techniques has been

proven to make them more of a snare and delusion than a real help. Approach systems improvement as you would taste a strange food—take a small bite, chew it thoroughly and pause to digest it to determine any possible ill effects. Take another bite only if no nausea, cramps or diarrhea occur.

Peerless Topman Says . . .

"Get a complete system; people need it to control manufacturing. Keep it simple and it will work better and be less trouble."

Specific Plans Needed

To provide a basis for planning and control, many detailed plans are needed. These should be developed as part of an integrated master plan, using the formal system to tie them all together.

Here are seven important plans, goals and objectives:

1. Customer demand forecasts: totals of all demands, subtotals for product families and major customers, subtotals for make-to-stock and make-to-order products and details for individual products including replacement or service parts and components for affiliated companies or plants

2. Build plans or master schedules: quantities of products and components indicating when they are to be produced and how many will be made

3. Plant output rates: for your plant and your principal vendors, to support the master schedule

4. Customer service levels: defining acceptable in-stock or on-time delivery performance

5. Productivity: including a variety of manpower and machinery utilization rates, major expense items and other manufacturing performance measures

6. Inventory levels: totals and subtotals by product family, inventory class or other useful categories

7. Record accuracy levels: acceptable error rates in on-hand and on-order balances, bills of material, customer order files, work-in-process details and cost data

Above all else, if they are to contribute to effective control, objectives must be consistent and achievable. They must be set by management with consideration for the trade-offs, the "least worst choices." A detailed discussion of each of these is beyond the scope of this book. The Bibliography gives sources of additional information for managers desiring in-depth coverage. Because of its importance, because of many existing misconceptions and fallacies and because of the lack of good references, we believe more discussion of record accuracy is both warranted and necessary. It will be found in Chapter 8 with other important support activities.

Setting Goals and Tolerances

In addition to establishing specific objectives, it is up to management to decide what variances are acceptable without corrective action. A basic flaw in most financial controls is that they report all variances, whether or not they are acceptable and whether or not a rational manager will deem it necessary to take corrective action. They produce an overwhelming volume of variances that must be sorted out by those responsible for controlling. These people must make their own decisions *at the time of each report* on which variances are significant and which are acceptable. The result is inevitably lost time, wasted effort, delayed or ignored actions and uneven control effectiveness. The effectiveness of a control system is greatly enhanced if variances are reported only on those plans where action is necessary. The validity of *management by exception* is well established.

Managers go wrong in two opposite ways in setting goals and tolerances. They either set them arbitrarily, with little or no real understanding of the trade-offs involved, or try to get scientific with elaborate mathematical calculations, as if such precision could be valid. The right answer is somewhere between the extremes.

Forecasts will be wrong. Strangely enough, past forecast errors are the best estimates of future ones and provide the needed tolerances. Statistical techniques keep academicians and consultants busy writing about them and testing various models but only rarely provide better information than a management team's collective judgment. This is particularly

Peerless Topman Says . . .

"Spend more time defining tolerances than establishing goals for manufacturing activities and inventories. This can make or break you."

true for product line totals, new product introductions and business cycle upturns and downturns.

The master schedule cannot be produced automatically by a computer. It must be hammered out as a compromise among managers attempting to balance customer service, stability of employment, cash flow, capital investment and company growth considerations. Staying within one week of schedule is an acceptably executed plan.

Plant output rates needed to support the master schedule can be calculated as discussed in the Appendix. Precise calculations involving detailed process data and future projections of planned order releases are almost never warranted. There are too many demands on capacity from new and redesigned products, methods improvements, unexpected scrap and rework, record errors, machine breakdown and the like which cannot be planned. Why calculate 75 percent of your capacity needs precisely when you have no effective method by which to get the balance except by guessing. Rough-cut approaches are simple, quick and provide long-term averages.

Although capacity plans are, at best, good averages, tolerances should be fairly tight. Recovering from sizeable inadequacies and excesses is difficult and expensive; the plan should be met closely until the data proves wrong and is adjusted. This is probably the most critical and difficult of all controls to manage.

Customer service, productivity and related goals are best set by stating some desired percentage improvement over present levels. A good approach makes today's best performance tomorrow's standard.

Inventory goals can be set by sound rational techniques. These are covered in George Plossl's previous writings listed in the Bibliography as well as new approaches to be included in Chapter 8. As with capacity, tolerances should be tight to initiate quick recovery actions before departing too far from plan.

The best test for a properly-set tolerance is the number of action messages it generates: too many won't be used effectively and fail to distinguish the "vital few" from the "trivial many"; too few can let troubles get too far out of hand before sounding the alarm.

Sensing and Feedback

The frequency of measuring variances with sensing mechanisms and the timeliness of the data fed back are of utmost importance. Traditional monthly accounting data issued several days after the close of the accounting period are adequate only for historical recordkeeping; much more timely and frequent feedback is necessary for management control. If the data is for scorekeeping, take your time; if the players need it, get it fast. In either case, it will be far more useful if it's accurate. The best form of feedback is a written report highlighting only those variances requiring corrective action.

The Important Result—Corrective Action and Control

Pogo, the hero of a popular comic strip in the 1950's and '60's, used a famous comment which aptly describes the management team in most companies—"We have met the enemy and he is us." Sporting teams, where winners and losers are clearly defined, have long recognized the value of teamwork. "Team" hardly applies to most management groups: they resemble more the Roman gladiators in ancient days fighting among themselves for simple survival rather than combining to defeat an external foe.

Nothing can compensate for failing to execute plans, however sound. We believe this is so important that we have included a whole chapter on this subject, Chapter 11. Having all of the other elements of a good control system is of no use if corrective action is not taken promptly.

This does not mean constantly revising the plan, although the most ardent advocates of MRP and computer-based systems would lead you to think so by their stress on the *replanning capabilities* of such programs. *Cooperative efforts by the full management team to execute the plan are mandatory.* Top management's directive must be, "A sound plan, well executed." Revising the plan should be the last resort.

5

HANDLE NO. 2-INVENTORY INPUT/OUTPUT CONTROLS

The Causes of Inventory

Inventory results when inputs are not immediately matched by outputs. The most common examples are order quantities, manufactured or purchased, that exceed immediate need. The next most common are other quantities that arrive ahead of need to create *safety stocks*. Third are orders for manufactured items, called work-in-process, that require the passage of time to complete. Other examples include material being reworked, scrap not yet written off, almost-finished assemblies awaiting shortage items and the myriad of materials still on hand that were supposed to have been already shipped. Few, if any, of these excesses become so by intent. A sharp drop in requirements for an item will turn a reasonable three-months' supply into an untenable 30-months' supply. A *sick* inventory can always be explained by reviewing the orders that create it. The problem is not to try to prevent all such mishaps (it's impossible) but to detect them promptly and act quickly and forcefully to offset their effects on the totals. Inputs usually arrive in accordance with plan; outputs, unfortunately, rarely match the plan.

How Do You Really Control Inventories?

As discussed in Chapter 2, inventory is not a "happening" subject to the whims of some capricious god. Neither is its control a simple matter of ordering "the right amount of the right item at the right time." Inventory is controlled only by balancing totals of inputs and outputs: when inputs exceed outputs, inventory increases. Until outputs exceed inputs, inventory will not decrease. Inventory can still be held to budget even when actual outputs, i.e. shipments, are off budget if such output variances are detected promptly and action is taken quickly to adjust inputs, i.e. production. Control depends first on planning, measuring and controlling

Peerless Topman Says . . .

"Don't let preoccupation with all the details interfere with managing the total inputs and outputs to inventory."

totals and then on managing the individual items to conform to these totals. Like air travel, it's necessary to know where and when the airplanes are scheduled to go before individual passengers can plan their trips.

One of management's four major handles on inventory is this input/output relationship:

$$\begin{aligned} \text{Starting inventory} \quad & + \quad \text{Input (production)} \\ & - \quad \text{Output (shipments)} \\ & = \quad \text{Ending inventory} \end{aligned} \qquad \text{Eq. 5-1}$$

Rearranging the terms helps to focus attention on the changes and emphasizes the need for balancing:

$$(\text{Ending} - \text{Starting inventory}) = (\text{Input} - \text{Output}) \qquad \text{Eq. 5-2}$$

The first two terms, of course, measure desired inventory change from the beginning of some period to its end. The master plan will cover the fiscal or calendar year but measurements of progress and control require frequent reporting of year-to-date data and budgeting weekly or monthly changes in the future. For relating actual performance to budget, the basic control equation can be set up using variances of actual data from budgeted figures:

Starting inventory variance   +   Input variance   Eq. 5-3
                               −   Output variance
                               −   Ending inventory variance

   In those companies whose products are largely made to order, keeping track of the status of *bookings,* or the unshipped customer order *backlog,* becomes significant in managing this important factor. A similar relationship of inputs and outputs exists for this situation:

Starting backlog   +   Input (new orders)   Eq. 5-4
                    −   Output (shipments or production)
                    =   Ending backlog

   It takes very little imagination to see how similar *backlog* and *inventory* are in their requirements for control and how *input* and *output* in Equation 5-4 are exactly like their opposites, *output* and *input*, in Equation 5-1. There seems to be no need to spend time in detailing separately how input/output control works for this type of business.

   Too few companies really attempt to control the totals. Too many of these try to manage inputs, outputs and inventory individually and separately. Sales people watch actual customer orders and shipments vs. forecasts; manufacturing people chart purchases, direct labor and plant output vs. budgets; the controller's office publishes data on excess inventory. And they all believe that somebody else is at fault when the plan is blown. Control is elusive, an illusion, until all three—inventory, inputs and outputs—are tracked together and watched by everybody.

   The basic Input/Output Control Chart is shown in Figure 5-1. Total

Month	Jan.			Feb.			Mar.			Apr.		
	Bud.	Act.	Var.	Bud.	Act.	Var.	Bud.	Act.	Var.	Bud.	Act.	Var.
Starting Inventory		3000		2950	2980	30	2900	2905	5	2850	2860	10
+ Inputs	400	410	10	400	395	(5)	450	435	(15)	450		
− Outputs	450	430	(20)	450	470	20	500	480	(20)	500		
= Ending Inventory	2950	2980	30	2900	2905	5	2850	2860	10	2800		

Figure 5-1   Basic Input/Output Control Chart

inventories of $3 million are to be reduced by $50,000 each month to reach a year-ending inventory objective of $2 million. Four months' budget and three months' actual performance are shown.

Obviously, the year got off to a shaky start. January ending inventories were $30,000 over budget as a result of an excess input of $10,000 and output being $20,000 less than planned. A substantial recovery was made in February; input was $5,000 less than budget, output $20,000 over target, leaving inventories only $5,000 above plan. In March, input was again reduced $15,000 under budget, but output fell off even more with a $20,000 variance, leaving inventories $10,000 above plan.

The cumulative inventory variance of $10,000 at the end of March is clear; it is not evident, however, whether input or output is the cause. This is always possible to determine by studying the monthly variances but there's a better way to show this useful information.

Input and output, along with inventories, can be shown as cumulative year-to-date figures using the format in Figure 5-2. It's easy to see that March inventories are $10,000 over budget even though year-to-date inputs were $10,000 less than budget because, in the same period, outputs were $20,000 less.

Month	Jan.			Feb.			Mar.			Apr.		
	Bud.	Act.	Var.	Bud.	Act.	Var.	Bud.	Act.	Var.	Bud.	Act.	Var.
Starting Inventory +		3000			3000			3000			3000	
Inputs −	400	410	10	800	805	5	1250	1240	(10)	1700		
Outputs =	450	430	(20)	900	900	0	1400	1380	(20)	1900		
Ending Inventory	2950	2980	30	2900	2905	5	2850	2860	10	2800		

Figure 5-2   Cumulative Input/Output Control Chart

Figures 5-1 and 5-2 are the two most commonly used formats for intput/output information. In both, columns would be included for future months covered in the overall budget showing the latest budgeted figures. It is well to have both: Figure 5-1 shows what is happening period-by-period and Figure 5-2 provides net changes year-to-date. The data can even be combined in one chart, saving paper at the risk of losing control. The important point is seeing the whole relationship clearly, finding out you're off course before it's too late to get back on and setting totals which then provide limits for the detailed decisions.

These reports, of course, show only the tips of the icebergs. It is well to have at least two levels of supporting data to explain significant variances. For top management in a multi-division corporation the input/ output chart would show the corporate totals supported by separate charts one level down for groups of companies and two levels down for individual companies. Each company would have its charts supported by data for product families and, possibly, for make-to-stock and make-to-order products in each family. Executives at each level would use the data to direct and measure their subordinates and would know in advance what explanation their seniors would require and how well they were doing their own jobs.

Input and Output Defined

The detailed factors included in input, output and inventory data vary from company to company. The principal inputs are productive labor and purchased materials and the principal outputs are shipments, called *sales* in many companies. To keep the numbers consistent with financial data, it is usual to attach associated burden to manufacturing labor; this is sometimes described as *loaded labor*. If not attached to labor, burden should be reported as an item on its own, particularly if it is too large to be included in any catchall "other" or "miscellaneous" item.

Purchased material input usually includes only direct materials. Factory and office supplies and other purchases like capital equipment and services are not included; these require separate controls. Sales usually include only those items actually shipped and billed to a customer, and thus transferred to accounts receivable, or shipped and charged to an affiliated operation.

Care must be taken that all items are valued on the same cost basis. This usually means that all, including sales, will be reported at *standard*. To account for all items which do not clearly belong to one of the major categories, another grouping is needed. This catchall, balancing or closing item is usually called *other inputs and outputs.* These modifications are shown in the Summary Input/Output Control Chart in Figure 5-3.

The inclusion of the "other" category may not be necessary if it is a small factor but even small variances at times can become significant and troublesome. Typical of such is *inventory reserves,* usually a forecast by financial people of how much inventory will be *lost* during the year. This is really another class of inventory. One purpose of setting up such reserves is to anticipate write-offs of obsolete materials. However, the most common function of the inventory reserve is to act as a hedge against the possibility that book inventory will not be in agreement with physical count at the end of the fiscal year. If there is valid evidence that inventory

Month	Jan.			Feb.		
	Bud.	Act.	Var.	Bud.	Act.	Var.
Starting Inventory + Purchased Material + Loaded Labor − Sales + Other Inputs and Outputs = Ending Inventory						

Figure 5-3 Summary Input/Output Control Chart

on hand at year-end is not the same as book value at that time, a correction can be made to the book value usually by transferring funds from the reserve account, or, rarely, to it, leaving total net inventories and net earnings undisturbed.

The determination and management of appropriate reserves can have a significant impact on total inventory. The size of a reserve is largely a matter of judgment, attempting to estimate how far the financial inventory data will be out of step with the physical inventory reality. Developments during the year will alter such estimates and these changes must be included in the inventory budgets and input/output control charts. It is important that top management know how their particular accounting system handles reserves. Their amounts and changes are just as much a part of the formal inventory plan as any other input or output.

A far better approach, however, is to eliminate the need for inventory reserves except for materials made obsolete by technological changes. Other reserves are unnecessary if there is one combined reporting system instead of separate financial and physical inventory records and if the formal systems records are accurate. It's a real tragedy, and an expensive one, when companies maintain two systems, one to keep track of dollars of inventory and the other to record pieces, pounds, gallons, etc. of materials separately, with different transactions to update each system. Set up one system for both, get the records accurate and eliminate the *annual write-off*.

Peerless Topman Says . . .

"Set up only one inventory accounting system, handling the dollars and also the pieces, pounds, gallons, etc. with the same transactions."

Another use of reserves is to phase in a change in standard costs gradually over a period of several months to avoid major changes being made immediately in important control data. The total adjustment due to the cost change can be made to the gross inventory book values immediately with that same amount added to reserves so that net inventory remains unchanged. In each of the following months, a portion of the addition can be transferred from reserves to inventory until the change is absorbed fully and the inventory restated in the new standards. The resultant apparent gradual increase in inventory must be understood by operating management and differentiated clearly from labor and material input or sales output effects.

It may be helpful to set up another account, particularly common in government contracts, called *progress payments*. These cover amounts advanced periodically by the customer to the vendor to reimburse the vendor for purchases of material and work expended on a contract. They have the effect of reducing the supplier's investment and risk in inventory and should be included in input/output control charts.

When using input/output charts, detailed supporting information will be needed to explain significant changes in the totals of purchased materials, loaded labor, sales and others. It may be helpful to keep track separately of internal transfers, the receipt of goods or services from an affiliated plant, to distinguish them from materials procured from outside sources. It also may be useful to distinguish material purchased for resale from goods processed in one's plant which have different burden structures.

Labor inputs can also be subdivided usefully. In-plant manufacturing labor and field installation labor are usually significantly different, follow different patterns of activity and have different burden rates. Output supporting details may, like material input, include internal transfers and material for resale. Some companies sell engineering, repair or other consultative services which can be reported separately. It may even be desirable to establish an intermediate level of output, such as *transfers to finished goods* and show input to and output from finished goods only on a separate report. Cosmetics and toiletries manufacturers may find *customer returns* a significant factor to break out of the total input to finished goods.

1. Starting Inventory
2. INPUTS
3.   Internal Transfers
4.   Material Purchased—Productive
5.   Material Purchased for Resale
6.   Material Burden
7.   Labor—Productive
8.   Burden
9.   Installation—Material & Labor
10.   Customer Engineering
11.   Other Inputs
12. TOTAL INPUTS (Lines 3 through 11)
13. OUTPUTS
14.   Internal Transfers
15.   Sales (except Resales)
16.   Resales
17.   Customer Engineering
18.   Other Output
19. TOTAL OUTPUT (Lines 14 through 18)
20. CHANGE IN GROSS INVENTORY (Line 12 − Line 19)
21. CHANGES
22.   In Reserves
23.   In Progress Payments
24. TOTAL CHANGES (Lines 20 through 23)
25. CHANGE IN NET INVENTORY (Line 20 − Line 24)
26. ENDING INVENTORY (Line 1 + Line 25)

Figure 5-4   Complete Input/Output Data

The secret of control is planning and measuring as many categories of inventory as are significant to the middle-level managers making decisions which influence input and/or output. Obviously, these managers will need far more detailed information than the higher-level managers to whom they report. Input/output reports should be structured to give each level only the detail it needs. Figure 5-4 lists the data in a report used by each of about 150 subsidiary companies, combined into about 12 group reports and then summarized in one final corporate report. Corporate management gets the summary with a brief explanation of the important variances in the groups not meeting plan. Group management receives their group's summary with details on individual company's problems. Individual company reports are supported by several pages of detail with further breakdowns of the data reported.

Staff Contributions to Top Management

The top management input/output report in any of the forms shown here will generate a series of management questions, all concerning why. To facilitate their review, these questions should be anticipated and answers prepared by staff people combining explanations by the companies' operat-

Peerless Topman Says . . .

"Challenge all inventory changes on the basis that all decreases are good and all increases bad unless clearly proven otherwise."

ing management with analysis and comments by the corporate staff. This is done every month at ITT for a General Managers' Meeting where Evert Welch played the staff role for many years. Every company in ITT makes a detailed report of performance compared to its master plan. Included in this is the status of inventory vs. budget, sales vs. forecasts and profits vs. plan. Input/output reports similar to Figure 5-4 are preferred.

Provided beforehand with these reports for all companies, the ITT staff prepares a meaningful summary for top management review and directed action. A general truism is recognized by all: *inventory increases are bad and decreases are good.* The first question that comes up each month is, "Did ending inventories increase or decrease and by how much?" This usually raises questions about such issues as changes year-to-date in inventories and sales, and how these compare to last year's data. All of these provide good background information and the input/output reports make it easy to determine which groups and which companies are contributing significantly to change. Usually, the basic company reports supply supporting information as to why. The next, more important, question is, "What is the total variance to budget (or forecast or plan) and how did it change during the previous month?". Again, the input/output reports are invaluable in tracing causes of and responsibility for changes.

By far the most frequent offender causing inventory increases will be underforecast sales. When this happens, top management's immediate question must be, "What's being done to reduce input?". This should require specific answers and actions; explanations such as, "The condition is only temporary and will remedy itself next month," should not be accepted. Every sales falldown or production delay of significance should initiate immediate changes in the master plan and the Master Production Schedule with adjusted input, output and inventories to match.

Another common cause of inventory increases is receipts in excess of the purchased material input plan. For many reasons, vendors frequently are not notified of reschedules when changes in program are made and buyers are often reluctant to enforce reschedules on a vendor even when the vendor has been notified. Improved management and control of purchased materials and their lead times is a very fruitful field, discussed in detail in Chapter 7.

All control starts with a plan. Every inventory increase indicates that total input exceeded output; every inventory decrease shows that total input was less than output. Obviously, most companies' plans include some inventory changes: control requires determining, first, if the change was more or less than planned and, second, what caused the variances from plan in input and output. Analyzing an inventory change involves identifying what input and output increases and decreases occurred and the causes.

The most common inputs are purchased material receipts, labor and burden additions and transfers of material from a lower level inventory. Other transactions that increase inventory are transfers from reserves and from progress payments. The most common output is sales where the product value is transferred from inventory to accounts receivable after shipment to a customer. Others include transfers of material from an inventory to one at a higher level and transfers to reserves and progress payments. Some accounting systems allow booking of so-called pseudo sales, often referred to as *accrued sales,* without transfer to accounts receivable to give a manufacturing operation credit for the completion of work even though title transfer is delayed.

Some manufacturing practices make it difficult to input in proper balance with output. In multiproduct manufacturing, the effects of producing in batches tends to balance out, even over short periods of time. But in many companies an input and its matching output do not occur on a daily or even weekly basis, leading to transient inventory changes. Input to raw material and purchased parts inventory occurs in lumps as orders are received; outputs are generally smoother over time. Input to work-in-process tends to be smoother than output which occurs in batches. Input to many stocked finished goods is frequently in large batches while output is smoother. But products made to order or sold in sets usually have the opposite effects. A locomotive or ship requiring a year to manufacture will be an extremely "lumpy" output. Because of this it is helpful to maintain and compare input and output on a cumulative as well as a periodic basis. The proof of the pudding is whether or not significant changes are detected promptly. Some businesses with long lead time products and annual programs can have input and output so offset in time that comparison of each to plan or budget is about the only meaningful approach.

Some input and output demand top management's continuous attention because changes are matters of judgment rather than reflecting operating variations under rules and policies. For example, reserves can be managed or even manipulated to achieve a particular effect on inventory. If there is heavy pressure to reduce it, increasing reserves is a very easy way out. More commonly, management pressures to keep reported profits high can cause transfers from a particular reserve account, resulting in an apparent increase in inventory.

A most questionable manipulation can be practiced with modern standard cost systems. You can manufacture inventory not actually needed simply to show increasing profits by over-absorbing burden costs. In standard cost systems, each dollar of direct labor going into inventory is accompanied by some fixed amount of burden. If the actual total burden generated in the accounting period is less than was transferred, the burden is over-absorbed and a profit (sometimes called "manufacturing profit") equal to the difference goes straight to the bottom line. The effect is to mortgage the future by reporting profits today not expected to result until some later period when the inventory will be needed. The distortion of input and output control data is obvious.

Another questionable practice to get the same effect is booking sales that cannot yet be consummated in an action called *accrued billings.* This is usually used where the customer has delayed the required delivery date for a large contract but the factory has already completed the job. Another is the shipment of product ahead of schedule, near the end of a critical profit period, so that the sales, profits and reduced inventory can be claimed. If the customer refuses to accept delivery, the transactions can be reversed in a future, less critical period.

Peerless Topman Says . . .

"Beware of changes in inventory caused only by bookkeeping. Numbers on paper respond much more readily than physical materials and plants to manipulation."

Individually, any of these activities can be defended as justified at some particular moment. But, so can casual borrowings from petty cash. Because they can seriously handicap sound inventory control, top management has the responsibility to define to what degree, if any, such practices will be condoned. Demanding the identification and reporting of specific input and output will go a long way toward minimizing the occurrance of well-meant but damaging manipulations.

Input/Output Control Applications

The applications of input/output controls are so varied that it is impossible to discuss them all. We can, however, discuss some alternatives and describe a few specific applications. The major, and some minor, inputs and outputs were discussed earlier and others will be obvious to the experienced manager. For control, inputs may be compared directly to outputs or each may be compared individually to budget or plan. Only changes in inventory may be reported or the data may show also the resultant inventory totals. Only input, output and inventory variances may be reported by periods although cumulative totals are likely to be more useful.

Many reporting units can be used. Physical units, where inventory groups permit them, are the clearest and most precise. Dollar totals, are, of course, the commonest unit of measure, permitting grouping of all kinds of inventory but suffering serious problems from inflation and standard vs. actual accounting definitions. Where materials are common, *standard hours* of labor can be very useful.

One of the most common and useful input/output control reports is the PSI (production-sales-inventory) report, generally used for finished goods inventories of consumer products such as TV sets, refrigerators, air conditioning units, etc. Figure 5-5 shows a typical report where the data are expressed in product units. In this case, production over the eight-

Time Period		1	2	3	4	5	6	7	8
"P" (Production)									
Planned	Period	700	800	600	900	800	800	1000	700
	Cumulative		1500	2100	3000	3800	4600	5600	6300
Actual	Period	700	700	400	1000	800	900	900	600
	Cumulative		1400	1800	2800	3600	4500	5400	6000
Variance	Period		−100	−300	+100		+100	−100	−100
	Cumulative		−100	−300	−200	−200	−100	−200	−300
"S" (Sales)									
Planned	Period	700	800	700	900	900	800	1000	800
	Cumulative		1500	2200	3100	4000	4800	5800	6600
Actual	Period	600	800	600	800	800	700	1000	700
	Cumulative		1400	2000	2800	3600	4300	5300	6000
Variance	Period	−100		−100	−100	−100	−100		−100
	Cumulative		−100	−200	−300	−400	−500	−500	−600
"I" (Inventory)		Starting Inventory—2300 Units							
Planned		2300	2300	2200	2200	2100	2100	2100	2000
Actual		2400	2300	2100	2300	2300	2500	2400	2300
Variance		+100		−100	+100	+200	+400	+300	+300

Figure 5-5   PSI Report

week period fell short of plan by 300 units, sales were 600 units below target and inventory, as a result, was above budget by 300 units, although actually the same as the beginning figure; the planned inventory reduction of 300 units did not materialize. Sales and production were equal over the period.

Material Input Control

Some important and useful reports of this type may not combine the three factors of input, output and inventory in order to give more detailed attention to one of them. Individual factor reports, however, must never be viewed as substitutes for the PSI report. As an example, sales may want a report comparing actual sales with those forecast by customers or in-product groups without detailing the related inventory or production data. Manufacturing also likes to see how their output relates to plan in sufficient detail to monitor individual plants or production areas for the purpose of highlighting bottlenecks.

Another important one-element control is on purchased material input. Most companies have or can easily get a *commitment report,* an identifiable plan for total receipts of purchased items. Few project the data beyond firm orders and even fewer monitor what is actually happening against that plan. Control of this can be exerted with a minimum of adverse impact on one's own manufacturing operations. Embarrassed by the number of changes in their delivery schedules, many purchasing agents are reluctant to insist that vendors honor revised dates. Purchasing people tend to take sides with the vendor and sympathize with the vendor's difficulties, particularly if they consider some demands unreasonable. Top management, aware of their own need for responding to unreasonable customer requests, must be insistent that purchasing at times make unreasonable demands of vendors.

A most effective handle for top management is monitoring total material inputs compared to actual needs.

Input/Output Aids to Inventory Forecasting

In one corporation, an elaborate, sophisticated and successful input/output report has been in continuous operation for about 13 years, with several hundred companies reporting to corporate headquarters every month. In summary, each report shows the top-level inputs and outputs for the current month compared to the most recent forecast, plus forecasts of these inputs, outputs and resulting inventory balances for the following three months. The report, shown in Figure 5-6, was originally designed when it became apparent that most companies miss year-end inventory forecasts by wide margins and do little better in the near term. It was recognized that inventory forecasts would be improved if they were based on forecasts of the contributing inputs and outputs. The form includes material, purchased parts, labor and burden inputs and sales and other

Month

Starting Inventory

Inputs

    Purchased Materials & Parts
    Direct Labor
    Burden
    Other
    Decreases in Reserves
    Decreases in Progress Payments
    Other Inputs
    Total Inputs

Outputs

    Sales
    Indirect Materials
    Increases in Reserves
    Increases in Progress Payments
    Other Outputs
    Total Outputs

Month-Ending Inventory

Figure 5-6   Input/Output Forecast

outputs and is tailored to the needs of the individual companies. For example, companies with significant field installation work forecast installation labor and the corresponding sales separately. Where consignments account for substantial portions of inventory change, their input and output are reported separately. If issues from small tool inventories are substantial or there are separately defined engineering accounts, these are included. In all cases, changes in reserves and, where applicable, progress payments are also accommodated.

In each month, forecasts are made for each of the three succeeding months in complete detail. The results have been very revealing. It should be fairly easy to forecast labor and burden and to predict reserve adjustments only three months ahead. Purchased material input should be reasonably well known over that period. Variations in sales might be expected to be the major unknown. Surprisingly enough, the expected *constants* refuse to hold still. A lot has been learned from the introduction of this control about what management does and does not know about the conduct of its business. These monthly reports continue to be a constant source of interesting data on the conduct of many of the several hundred businesses covered.

6
HANDLE NO. 3—
THE MASTER PRODUCTION
SCHEDULE

The Master Plan and Production Plan

A *master plan* is an integration of all the operating plans for the conduct of a business, providing the music so that all management sings the same song. It incorporates and reconciles objectives for Manufacturing, Sales, Marketing, Engineering and Finance Departments, develops levels of capital expenditures, manpower, equipment utilization and all other budgeted variables. Successful management reviews both the master and supporting detailed plans on a regular and continuing basis, at least monthly, revising when needed to provide the best operating plans for the future. The master plan is used initially to develop the original annual budgets for all departments as well as their detailed operating plans: subsequent changes are incorporated as revised budgets. Budgets and their preparation are detailed in Chapter 8.

Manufacturing's portion of the master plan is called the *Master Production Schedule*. Of utmost importance is the recognition of any material or capacity limitations that would make the master production schedule impossible or impractical to achieve. It must portray a feasible program that will achieve management's objectives on inventory levels, customer service, operating costs and stability of employment while considering also new products and design changes to existing products, new plants and equipment, changes in distribution systems and other significant factors.

A basic concept of modern production management is that the master production schedule be reviewed constantly and revised (hopefully as a last resort) when necessary. Changes are then translated into revised, detailed manufacturing and inventory plans.

Peerless Topman Says . . .

"Don't tolerate a master production schedule which is a wish list. It must be buildable and billable."

The master production schedule states specifically *what* is to be produced, *how much* of it is to be made and *when*. It should contain data on everything to be produced, including finished products, intermediates, service parts, components for affiliated plants, etc. It is not the sales plan of shipments or the marketing forecast of customer demand, but it is developed to support both. The formal systems supporting it generate plans for the specific resources of men, money, materials and machinery needed. It must be cognizant of all pending significant developments in products and processes. Capacity and capital limitations will have been taken into consideration along with the availability of materials and services, technical problems and any other constraints on the company's ability to produce. A good master production schedule will be the result of a real team effort among Marketing, Sales, Manufacturing, Engineering and Finance to arrive at the best possible compromise among their conflicting interests. It ties all the departmental plans together, becoming the hub of the production plan.

As was discussed in Chapter 4, the master production schedule drives the material requirements plan to generate orders for both purchased and manufactured items needed to support the production plan.

The master schedule is most effective when supported by such a detailed plan but is both necessary and useful even before a working material requirements planning program is available. It also supplies inputs directly to the *capacity requirements plan* to determine *what, how much,* and *when* manpower, machines and plant facilities will be needed and provides information to the *financial plan,* whose *what* is money, to help decide *how much* and *when* it will be needed.

The master production schedule is the basis for all manufacturing control. It is management's most comprehensive handle on the business. The soundness of the basic operating plans and the effectiveness with which they are executed will depend on the management team's understanding of, and experience in, managing the master production schedule.

The Development of a Master Production Schedule

The master production schedule is only rarely made up directly of customer orders on-hand and forecasts of future demand. Production batch quantities frequently differ from shipping lots, some customer demand may be filled from inventory without replenishment, and seasonal sales patterns may be met from level production.

For material planning, the master production schedule must extend over a horizon far enough into the future to cover the longest manufacturing cycle and, hopefully, all raw and purchased material procurement. For capacity planning, it should extend at least a year. It is important for top management to appreciate that there is no alternative to forecasting production over this period of time. Failure to provide for it in the formal system will simply result in a myriad of independent *forecasts* made by personnel making daily decisions who are neither authorized nor competent to consider the important factors involved.

In many businesses, the product defined in the master production schedule is often quite different from the one actually delivered to the customer. When the customer can make a selection from a variety of products, the master production schedule may be stated in terms of base machines, accessories, attachments or even in sets of parts, such as the air conditioning equipment on an automobile, associated with options to be made available to the customer. The choice of the particular level in the bills of material at which the master production schedule is to be generated, how these bills are to be structured, how orders and forecasts are to be blended and how excessive "nervousness" is to be avoided are an important part of the growing lore of manufacturing control.

This power to alter the game plan to suit the game situation is undoubtedly as necessary and valuable in manufacturing as in any sport.

Like all power, however, it can easily be abused. Failure of management to recognize the limitations, costs and penalties of changing the master production schedule, particularly in the near term, can lead to "nervous prostration" of the system. Among the toughest decisions management

Peerless Topman Says . . .

"Put strong restrictions on tinkering with the master production schedule. It can easily cost far more than it's worth."

must make is the degree of flexibility allowable between unlimited changes and no changes. Both extremes are wrong. The best answer will vary with the time span and with the type of business but will always be a moderate compromise.

Uses of the Master Production Schedule

The master production schedule is the key to all resource planning. In the short-range, it can define the best utilization of available manpower, machines and materials. Over intermediate periods, it can develop the needed capacity, manufacturing schedules and materials procurement information. For the long-range, it can provide pertinent information on the need for new plants, additional machinery and capital requirements or the need for the orderly reduction of present facilities.

Probably the best known use of the master production schedule is as the input to the material requirements plan for material control. Through a rigorously logical process, the master production schedule is translated via bills of material into details of *what, how much* and *when* each manufactured and purchased component is required. For those interested, material requirements planning and ordering techniques are explained in the Appendix.

More recently, the real value and importance of using the master production schedule in the determination of capacity requirements has come into sharper focus; capacity planning and control are among the most active subjects under study by manufacturing control practitioners. They provide the means to achieve better balancing of work center outputs and to control lead times. This function, the missing link in the control systems of most manufacturing companies, is covered in detail in the Appendix.

One of the most difficult tasks in business—making valid customer delivery promises—is based on, at worst, intuitive, seat-of-the-pants decisions, on time formulas or, at best, on a detailed review of one order at a time, with little or no understanding of the total impact of all orders. Very few companies can make and meet delivery promises consistently enough to inspire confidence on the part of their customers. Distrust between buyer and seller leads to hedging practices on both parts; buyers specify unnecessarily-early delivery requirements and sellers make whatever promise they believe necessary to get the order, creating a wide credibility gap expensive to both. The master production schedule provides the basis for making believable customer promises and for negotiating mutually profitable terms when significant changes in order deliveries are requested.

Using the master production schedule to make valid delivery promises to customers is illustrated in Figure 6-1. Customer orders are recorded when received as *bookings* in the proper time period, then subtracted from the master schedule quantities and a balance of product uncommitted to specific orders is maintained. The detailed manufacturing plan supporting the master production schedule will highlight promptly all failures to adhere to supporting material schedules and also show up inadequate capacity situations jeopardizing adherence to the master schedule and the consequent inability to meet promised deliveries.

Week	1	2	3	4	5	6	7	8
Master Production Schedule		50		50		60		60
Bookings		50		38		21		7
Uncommitted		—		12		39		53

Figure 6-1   Customer Delivery Promises Via The Master Production Schedule

Additional new orders will consume the uncommitted portions of the master schedule. Customers' requests for delivery can be evaluated by analyzing the few real alternatives. For example, suppose a customer requests delivery of 15 units of the product covered by Figure 6-1 in week 4. There are only three choices:

- Agree to the request, using three units now promised to some other, less "equal" customer and rescheduling that customer to week 6

- Agree to the request, increasing the total number of units scheduled in week 4 to 53

- Promise a split shipment of 12 in week 4 and three in week 6

The risks are obvious. The first and third alternatives may cause some customer dissatisfaction. The second may cost a significant amount over the previous plan. Of course, it should not be offered as a valid alternative until a detailed check proves it is feasible and identifies such excess costs. Where products are similar, with many common components, a fourth alternative may be available. *Swap* components by decreasing the master schedule for one to permit a corresponding increase in that for another, thus minimizing the potential excess costs.

Utilizing this approach, companies are able to have order entry, marketing and sales personnel make valid delivery promises to customers immediately on receipt of orders where no tough or expensive choices are involved. Several of these companies are able to command premium prices for their products, especially for deliveries made in shorter than normal industry periods.

It's impossible to over-emphasize the beneficial effects of good budgets on the total management of the business. The master production schedule, representing as it does the consensus of all managers on how the business should be operated, provides a rational, methodical approach to budgeting. The advantages of replacing former practices using estimates based on past ratios, industry data or competitors' figures or making wishful guesstimates are obvious. The inventory budget developed from the material requirements plan can define specifically how much inventory is enough, as detailed in Chapter 8. Equally valid budgets for direct and indirect labor, purchased material commitments, cost of goods sold, cash flow and sales income can be developed rigorously from the master production schedule. Profit projections follow directly from such budgeting. Equally important, these approaches also provide management with the ability to assess the specific effects on various budgets of significant changes in operating plans.

A good master production schedule is also the best measure of the factory's performance in meeting basic plans. Past practices were limited to measuring performance against subordinate targets such as setup time, machine and labor utilization, output rates, use of supplies and a myriad of overhead costs. Now the factory's all-important adherence to the overall schedule can be measured and responsibility for fall-downs clearly assigned to whatever department—Manufacturing, Engineering or Marketing—may be contributing.

Engineers have long considered their work to be a creative, inventive art form and have resisted performance schedules as impractical. Involving them in master production scheduling will show engineering clearly the compelling need to define the *what, how much* and *when* of new designs. The schedule provides the means to predict and measure the impact of their falldowns on the total business. Engineering can and should become as responsive a part of the manufacturing process as any other department. Good control of manufacturing will be severely handicapped if they are not.

By far, the most important attribute of the master production schedule is its ability to make possible a consensus, a workable compromise among the various management factions having differing ambitions and goals. Marketing sees its primary objective as generating the maximum in flow of customer orders and usually feels no responsibility for excess inventories, idle capacity or for deciding which customers will not be served when capacity is overloaded. Manufacturing is most concerned with inventory, costs and production efficiency, with little real appreciation for the importance of customer service. Engineering concentrates single-mindedly on designing newer and better products and produces its output—bills of material—in the form it likes rather than in a format adapted to the needs of other users. Finance is preoccupied with profit planning, cash flow, capital needs and the state of the order backlog, accompanied by a perpetual curiosity as to why good plans never seem to materialize and accepted budgets are rarely met. In most businesses, these groups behave as if they were in competition; their relations are characterized by mutual distrust. "Teamwork for the good of the company" is a hollow phrase. This dismal picture is not the result of the perversity of man or some evil competitor's plot but rather the lack of common goals more definitive than profits.

What's needed is a common plan to which all can agree, specifying mutual activities to which each can contribute and showing clearly the benefits of teamwork. The master production schedule provides this common plan. Agreed to by all, the contribution of each and their interrelations are clearly defined and the performance of each in meeting their shared responsibilities can be measured. Marketing is responsible for getting the orders it agreed were obtainable and obviously necessary to support the schedule. Manufacturing is responsible for producing the output it agreed was realistic within the accepted limits of flexibility. Obviously both will fail to meet their responsibilities fully at some times. When this happens it's necessary to do more than identify and chastise the culprit.

Peerless Topman Says . . .

"Use your master plans and schedules to get all departments singing to the same music instead of pointing fingers at each other."

The plan must be modified or the inevitable penalties of excess inventory and/or unhappy customers accepted. The data in Figure 6-1 also can be helpful in this situation. As week 4 comes closer, the question, "Will we sell *the total* in the master production schedule?" becomes pertinent. Again there are only a few real choices:

- assume the total will be sold, later if not in week 4, and continue to produce all the components, building and carrying excess inventory corresponding to the unsold portion

- assume the uncommitted balance will not be sold, reducing the master schedule and freeing up the material and capacity allocated to it for other uses, including delaying replenishment orders not needed until later

- some combination of both, reducing the master schedule to delay those components not already in inventory and accepting the excesses when it is too late to act

Admittedly these are difficult decisions to make. The important point is that they should not be made unilaterally by either Marketing or

Manufacturing, but by a joint effort with both fully aware of the cost and marketplace implications. The master production schedule makes this a practical way to approach the problem.

Engineering and Finance can also become vital parts of the act. Engineering must support both Manufacturing and Marketing and complete their work when the plan requires it. Finance knows what capital will be required, what cash flow needs will be and can easily find out what went wrong when the plan isn't met. Best of all, the effect of needed changes in the master production schedule on all individual department operations can be evaluated and sound compromises adopted. Coordinating the activities of managers is the most productive use of the master production schedule.

The development of internal expertise in this area is likely to be much more important than with any of the other more popular techniques. Those who must become expert are middle and upper level managers, many of whom, unfortunately, care little or nothing about becoming involved with production. The setting up and use of the master production schedule should be the subject of a management study in depth and may well justify the services of outside counselors who have had experience with the variety of approaches available. A widely overlooked subject for many years, master scheduling has gained considerable professional attention since the early 1970s. Fortunately, literature on the subject is growing by leaps and bounds, specialized technical seminars are being offered by consultants, universities and technical societies and experienced, competent counselors are emerging.

7

HANDLE NO. 4 –
LEAD TIME MANAGEMENT

Introduction

Among the many variables in manufacturing, lead time is the least understood and the most poorly managed. In fact, most managers do not believe that lead times can be managed at all; they view them as a variable with which they must live and try to cope. They see their only salvation in watching closely what is happening—measuring actual lead times—and developing a system capable of reacting quickly as they "tell it the truth" about the actual lead time.

Few managers underestimate the importance of dependable lead times in controlling manufacturing. All ordering techniques need a planned, average figure for each item, whether purchased or manufactured, to relate the release of replenishment orders to the time of receipt of the material. Managers differ in their desires for lead times. Manufacturing managers like longer lead times, associating them with a more stable operating plan, comfortable cushions of work-in-process and more time to recover from the inevitable upsets. Marketing managers like short lead times with quicker reaction to changes in customers' desires although they, too, prefer sizeable backlogs of orders as evidence of healthy business. Financial managers see clearly the direct relation between manufacturing lead times and the investment in work-in-process and would prefer much less; they're helpless to do much or suggest solutions, however.

The real truth about lead time is shocking. Although *practically every item manufactured today can be produced in normal batch quantities in a few hours,* companies continue to work with weeks and months of planned lead times for these items. Plagued by lack of raw materials, shortages of components and frequent interruptions in production, too many managers

Peerless Topman Says . . .

"See that lead times are managed; they can be. See that they are short; they should be."

believe the only practical solution is to allow longer planned lead times. Too few see clearly that this only contributes to more shortages and allows more time in which interruptions can occur. The truth about lead time is that *it will be what you say it is and it's always better to say it is shorter.* Obviously this needs explanation.

What Is Lead Time?

The usual answers to this question are "too long," "too erratic" or "too unpredictable," reflecting the frustration of the victims of unmanaged lead times. Before they can be managed, however, some terms must be defined clearly, some concepts must be understood and some misconceptions corrected.

The total time required to procure all raw materials and purchased components, process them, test and package the finished product is the *production cycle time.*

The total manufacturing time needed to perform all necessary operations in the plant from the start of the earliest to the completion of the last is the *manufacturing cycle time.*

Both of these are the sums of many individual item lead times. These are the elapsed times from the release of an order to buy or make the item until the material on the order is completed and ready for the next operation or for shipment to a customer. Using ordering techniques like MRP, as discussed in the Appendix, which indicate in advance when an order is to be released, it is not necessary to include in this lead time paperwork time to cover the time required to decide an order is needed. The term *lead time* thus applies to individual items, one at a time or collectively.

Planned, average lead times are needed for each component by the formal system to tell ordering how much time they need to allow between starting and finishing orders for purchased or manufactured items. These are made up of the following elements:

- setup time: changing over process equipment, machines or work centers

- running time: making the batch

- move time: transmitting it to the next work area or to storage

- queue time: waiting in line behind other orders to be processed

The sum of setup, running and move times is rarely more than a few hours for normal batches; expediters pushing orders through in response to president's edicts prove this every day.

Queue time, occupied in waiting and delays, accounts for the difference between productive work time and the weeks and months commonly used in lead times. *Mismanaged queues of work-in-process cause the problems of shortages and excess inventories which accompany erratic, unpredictable lead times.* Queues are necessary in manufacturing, except in continuous processing plants like petroleum refineries. Work in batch processing operations rarely, if ever, flows smoothly and some work-in-process is necessary to keep all operations busy, particularly when their production rates differ widely. Each work center, therefore, has some planned, average queue time which will apply to all orders passing through it. The advantages of balancing work centers and keeping work flowing smoothly are obvious—queues can be reduced, investment in work-in-process minimized, control of plant activities improved with far fewer open orders and lead times and cycle times improved. The benefits are enormous.

Actual, average work center queue times are the collective experiences of all individual orders processed in one work center in some period. For good control, actual and planned average queue times *must be the same.* Obviously this requires managing backlogs of work-in-process *in total* at each work center, balancing the input of new orders against output of completed work, *managing capacity.*

Actual order lead times are the specific experiences of individual orders from start to finish. Unlike work center queue times, planned and

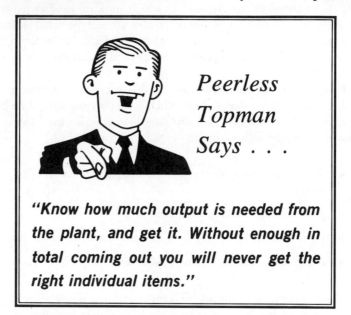

Peerless Topman Says . . .

"Know how much output is needed from the plant, and get it. Without enough in total coming out you will never get the right individual items."

actual order lead times should not be the same. You do not want each order for an item to require the same planned average lead time every time it is processed. Some times it will be ordered early—to level the load on a work center, for example. Some times it will be released late—reacting to a quantity problem or a forecast error. After it is in process, its completion date will change as customers request earlier or later delivery or for a myriad of reasons for changing schedules known to every manufacturing manager. For good control reacting to such changes, actual order lead times will need to be shorter or longer than the planned average. This requires *managing priorities.*

Managing lead times requires managing capacity, matching work center inputs and outputs to hold the planned average queues, and also managing priority, moving urgently needed orders to the head of the queue and letting unneeded orders wait. The real key is knowing how much capacity is needed—and getting it—and having valid priorities and following them. It is necessary and very beneficial to smooth the flow of work through the plant (yours and your suppliers) to minimize the need for cushions of work-in-process. Figure 7-1 shows the effect of reduced lead times on work-in-process investment.

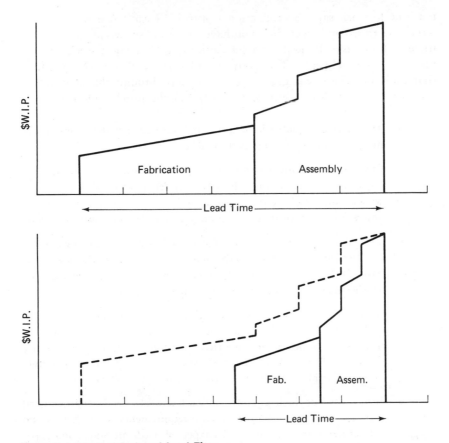

Figure 7-1 Effect of Reduced Lead Time

The Lead Time Syndrome—Invitation to Boom/Bust Cycles

At some time in every business it becomes obvious that the plant, or one or more work centers in it, cannot handle the amount of work required for completion in the stated lead times. The actual time to complete the work obviously will be longer than planned. The conclusion seems obvious— lengthen the lead times.

The sequence and the consequences are exactly the same, whether it involves orders placed by a Purchasing Department on a vendor or orders placed on an operating department by Production Control. In one case, the vendor says to Purchasing, "I can no longer deliver to a four-week lead time since it will take me six weeks to complete the orders I have now. I must increase my lead time. Six weeks is the minimum I need now; eight weeks would insure on-time delivery." In the other case, the screw-machine foreman says to Production Control, "I can't live with a four-week lead time any longer since you have given me six weeks' work. Let's increase lead time. It need six weeks minimum but eight weeks would insure on-time delivery." The words are identical and so is the certainty that both situations will get worse. Let's step through the sequence of events that will follow, concentrating first on the purchasing area:

- The supplier's quoted lead times are increased including some safety margin to insure on-time performance.

- Customers' ordering systems react, sooner or later, generating more orders in accordance with the new, longer-quoted lead times. Four weeks' extension of lead time will produce *at least* four weeks of new orders from each customer. *Evidence of a boom in the economy seems clear.*

- The suppliers' order backlog (bookings) will remain beyond the suppliers' ability to handle in the quoted lead time since the new orders have more than filled the additional time. It will be obvious that another increase plus a greater safety margin are needed.

- More new orders will be stimulated, *the gap between quoted and actual lead times will persist,* and another extension of lead times will be made—and another, and another. Customers, fearing a capacity crunch, will order in excess of real requirements and may even double-order and triple-order. *More evidence of a boom will appear.*

- Lead times—at the beginning, only a few weeks—will lengthen until they become a year or longer. Known requirements get more hazy and over-ordering more common. Unexpected needs are added and expedited but unneeded deliveries are rarely rescheduled or cancelled.

- At some point it will become apparent to the vendor that the real problem is capacity. With the recent high incoming rate of new orders and the large backlogs of unshipped orders, the vendor feels it is safe to make the needed investment. The volume of orders behind schedule is used to determine the needed increase and more capacity is put in place. *The boom is now over.*

- With increased capacity, promised due dates are being met. There is now no need to increase lead times. Customers' ordering slows down and general uneasiness arises about the possibility of a recession.

- Reduced lead times appear to be an obvious inducement to customers which will generate more business for a vendor and thus lessen the vendor's concern about the fall-off in new order rates and about keeping this new capacity busy. *The bust is beginning.*

- *New orders will probably not be stimulated* since customers' requirements for the lead time, in effect, have already been placed, usually overstated and sometimes double-ordered as a result of trying to outguess long lead times and poor delivery performance.

- The possibility of recession causes extreme pressure in customers' operations on cutting inventories fattened from the over-ordering and the poorly-defined priorities which are always a concommitant of long lead times.

- In addition, shortened lead times mean that some legitimate orders could now be cancelled and not replaced until later. Backlogs of bookings shrink as lead times shrink, even more rapidly than they expanded. *The bust is now in full swing.*

- Inevitably suppliers will recognize the need to slash capacity to match what appear to be apparent requirements. Lead times restabilize eventually somewhere near their original magnitude. *The bottom of the recession is reached.*

Exactly the same phenomenon will occur if a company adjusts its internal planned lead times in an attempt to close a gap between planned and actual figures. The reaction of systems is inescapable: when lead times increase, the system directs more orders to be released now; when lead times are cut, the system stops releasing orders.

People's normal reactions aggravate the cycle. When lead times increase they are less certain of their needs but are optimistic and order more, fearing to jeopardize their own ability to deliver. When lead times shrink they become more pessimistic of their own needs, more critical of ordering, more prone to reschedule or cancel orders. To these internal factors must be added external effects. Economists, academicians, technical journal editors and trade associations interpret new order and industry bookings and backlog data without considering the distortions introduced into these data by lead time changes. Booms and busts feed on themselves. The Lead Time Syndrome is related to a potent "disease"—amateurs tinkering with lead times.

We've seen this cause serious trouble in many companies' internal activities. Its ability to cause harm is made even more potent by responsive MRP programs on computers. It caused a disastrous depression in the semiconductor industry in 1974-76 although the true demand for these products had increased steadily since 1973. It periodically occurs in those industries which like to operate with small unused capacity reserves.

Castings, forgings, bearings, chain, glass bottles, alloy steels and many other similar products frequently experience this syndrome. Like leprosy, it can't be cured but we can hope to arrest its progress and alleviate its more crippling symptoms.

Peerless Topman Says . . .

"Be sure your people are inoculated against the Lead Time Syndrome. It's highly contagious, extremely harmful and long-lasting."

Treating the Lead Time Disease

The cure is very simple in concept but is extremely difficult in practice. Earlier we stated that manufacturing control requires the performance of three functions:

- Make a valid master production schedule
- Plan and control capacity to support it
- Plan and control priorities to use all resources effectively

Actual lead times are longer than planned because capacity has been recently inadequate. As a result backlogs of released orders or of actual material-in-process have grown in excess of planned levels. *Changing the planned lead time will not close this gap.* The only real solutions are:

- Get more capacity and work off the excess
- Reduce the master schedule to match available capacity

It should be obvious that tinkering with lead times cannot solve capacity problems. What is not obvious, but should be understood by every manager involved with decisions affecting procurement of materials, manufacturing operations and relations with customers, is that *long lead times make it impossible to plan and control priorities adequately.*

Techniques for planning and controlling capacity are not complex, expensive or difficult to install and operate. We need to determine how much capacity is needed to support the master schedule and then get it. This is equally true of both manufactured and purchased items. Customers need to talk more *in capacity terms* to their key vendors, particularly if and when the suppliers' capacity is limited or inflexible. The early ordering of more material will not insure getting an adequate total; it will insure poorer use of available capacity, meaning more shortages of wanted materials and, simultaneously, excess inventories of unneeded items.

When one of its vendors has capacity problems, a company must assure itself of enough capacity to satisfy the requirements of its master production schedule, or reduce the master schedule. And, the best way to assure the availability of needed capacity is to *buy capacity,* not just place part-number orders: buy hours of machine capacity, moulds of castings, gallons of chemicals, tons of metal, etc. in total quantities equal to total needs. Be sure how much capacity is needed and then get it, if not from regular suppliers, then from other suppliers.

When a plant work center has trouble making enough good products to support the master schedule, move promptly to increase its output to meet total needs. Internally, capacity can be increased only by the use of overtime, added people and work-shifts or subcontracting. Don't give that screw-machine foreman extra lead time; it will only create more work-in-process, added chaos and greater delinquencies. At all costs, hold planned lead times; refuse to allow increases. Make manufacturing combat the real problem, inadequate capacity.

Externally, insist on similar handling of vendors who want more lead times; solving capacity problems is the only solution that will help the company. It's good for the economy and for industry in general as well. Until purchasing agents understand the Lead Time Syndrome they will not know when it's best to say, "We're not going to give you orders further out. Get this much capacity for us and get yourselves back on schedule." Until marketing and suppliers recognize the futility of lengthening lead times, they won't realize the only workable approach is to say to their customers, "We don't want to receive more orders spread over longer periods. How much additional capacity do you need from us?"

The real problem in curing the lead-time disease is in getting the key people involved in procurement and manufacturing to accept the truth about lead time. It is counter-intuitive, against all their experience and common sense. *The lead time will be what you say it is* and, occasionally, when capacity is not adequate, plus a little more. Changing the planned lead time will not get rid of the "plus a little more." This can be eliminated only by changing capacity.

Fallacies about Lead Time

There are some common misconceptions about lead time which need correcting:

Fallacy: Lead times are independent variables beyond our control; the best we can do is get a fast, responsive material control system and frequently adjust the planned lead times to match the actual.

Truth: Lead times can be managed, in fact they must be. Every effort must be exerted to avoid changing planned lead times in the system to prevent excessive nervousness and to avoid the lead time syndrome which compounds the problem.

Fallacy: We need ways to calculate lead times more accurately, determine statistically how much they vary and provide safety stocks to overcome the effects of this variation.

Truth: The calculable elements (setup, running and move time) account for less than 15 percent of most lead times, planned and actual. Queue time is the biggest element, causing practically all the variation, and there is no way to calculate queue time scientifically. Adjusting safety stocks is self-defeating, leading also to the Lead Time Syndrome and excessive nervousness.

Fallacy: With a good priority planning and control technique like MRP a company can cope with varying lead times no matter how big the queues are.

Truth: Large queues mean long lead times, manufacturing cycle times and planning horizons. As shown in Figure 7-2, lengthening lead times will extend the horizon of the master production schedule, thus influencing orders already released, causing new orders to be triggered by needs farther out in the future and, consequently, less reliable, and keeping orders open longer making them more likely to need changing. Priorities can be valid only when queues are short.

Fallacy: Longer lead times are better, giving us more time to react, to handle the upsets we know are coming.

Truth: Longer lead times generate larger amounts of work-in-process by causing more orders to be released sooner, keeping them exposed longer to

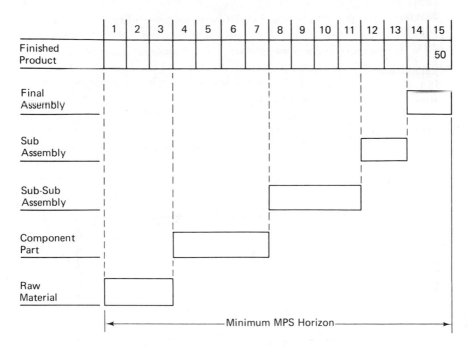

Figure 7-2 Effect of Lead Time on Planning Horizon

potential upsets. Engineering has more time to redesign the materials the plant is working on, more *happenings* can occur in the plant and more customers can change their minds. The manufacturing cycle is longer and the schedules issued to support it are less valid. The phrase, *long, dependable lead times*, is a contradiction in terms. Longer lead times will be more erratic; only short lead times can be reliable.

Fallacy: When actual lead times are longer than planned, there is no recourse except to tell the system the truth and increase the planned figures to match, or, better, to exceed the actual.

Truth: This is the most damaging fallacy of all. It not only fails to help solve the problem, it will inevitably aggravate it. The difference between planned and actual lead times will increase. This is the tragic effect of the Lead Time Syndrome.

Purchasing's Role in Managing Lead Times

Other than the unit price, the only impact on inventory made by a purchased item is the overall time between receipt into inventory and relief from inventory when it leaves the company as part of some end product. Since the Purchasing Department has no ability to control the flow of the item through the plant after it is received, its major responsibility in inventory management is to see that material does not get into inventory until the latest practical moment. This means seeing that suppliers meet requested due dates and effectively rescheduling orders already placed as well as placing new orders in time. Most purchasing people recognize clearly and respond quickly and effectively to the need to expedite urgently-needed materials, whether already on order with a vendor or not yet ordered. They understand priority control. Few, however, understand capacity planning and control and see any need to be concerned about a supplier's ability to meet their total needs. "That's his problem" is their stock reply. However, when *his* capacity is inadequate

Peerless Topman Says . . .

"Assign to Purchasing the job of buying vendor capacity to insure short procurement times as well as their normal task of buying materials and services."

the problem winds up being theirs—coping with increasing shortages and more frequent reschedules. The Lead Time Syndrome makes victims of both buyers and sellers. Purchasing's real role in managing lead times is to *work with vendors on both priority and capacity planning and control.* Every buyer should fight an increase in lead time at least as hard as an increase in price.

The Buyer-Seller Relationship

All of the problems of inter-departmental relationships within a manufacturing business among Marketing, Engineering, Finance, Quality Control, and Manufacturing Control raise their heads in the buyer-seller relationship. All of the production problems that arise within a company's own departments occur in dealing with a vendor. The two most important words in buyer-seller relationships are *mutual respect*.

How one chooses to organize solutions to these problems and develop this respect is a matter of diverse opinions. The proponents of complete vesting of all responsibility in dealing with vendors in a Purchasing Department see the advantages of a focal point for all matters affecting the vendor and also prefer that the vendor provide a similar function in its sales group. Others see advantages in eliminating from the Purchasing people's load many tasks which others can handle: for example, having the buyer's production control people talk about schedule changes to the seller's scheduling department, letting quality control people help vendors solve quality problems and in other ways getting Purchasing out of the middle, relaying messages from the vendor to which they contribute nothing. The principal gain is more time and resources in Purchasing applied to the big problem—finding better sources for adequate materials at lower prices.

There isn't any best answer to this question. Companies can operate successfully in the future using either approach, just as they have in the past. The important point is that adequate resources be assigned to perform the vital functions. Whichever way you go, a well-documented procurement manual describing these functions and how they will be handled will be invaluable to company personnel and to vendors alike.

However the functions are organized, the problem of vendors extending lead times as a result of capacity problems is certain to occur. It is in this environment of strained capacity and increasing vendor lead times that a real payoff can result from good vendor relations. A Purchasing organization wise enough to see the need and able to negotiate for capacity rather than parts, capable of helping a vendor understand that it is of mutual benefit, can contribute immeasurably to better customer service, reduced inventories and lower costs for its own company.

The Importance of Price

It takes a lot of judgment on the part of the procurement operation to determine when price should be the final determinant in placing a purchase order. Specifications are seldom so definitive and all-inclusive as to guarantee a usable product on the basis of their compliance alone. Staying with the same supplier may have definite advantages to the user. Ability to meet due dates and willingness to work cooperatively on subsequent schedule changes may be worth more than price differences. Getting an adequate share of the supplier's capacity may offset significant price differentials. Purchasing's job is to get the right price, certainly, but also to get enough in the shortest possible lead time.

8

IMPORTANT SUPPORTS FOR THE HANDLES

The Inventory Budget

In his book, *Profitability Accounting for Planning and Control* (Ronald Press, NY, 1963), Robert Beyer distinguishes three kinds of accounting: *custodial*—concerned with the business assets; *performance*—comparing actual vs. plan, and *decision*—involving the comparison of costs of alternative action. The first two can be termed scorekeeping and accountants are good at these, except for making reasonable plans or budgets. Little is done with the third—the one that would really help the players. This chapter deals with the second from the point of view of the players.

Most companies use a month-by-month annual budget for sales and net income but do not necessarily budget other important factors in their businesses on that same month-by-month basis. It is difficult, if not impossible, to meet profit goals without a well-managed inventory budget. At the very least, there has to be an estimate of what will happen to inventory as sales vary while inputs of material and labor remain relatively fixed. Figure 8-1 shows the usual format for an inventory budget. Some factors may not be relevant in many businesses and would be omitted.

It is necessary that there be a mechanism for top management approval of all important budgets before they become official. Under the best of circumstances, factors of importance will be overlooked in preparing budgets and lead to awkward explanations of variances. Therefore,

	Budget	Actual

Raw Material
Purchased Parts
Manufactured Parts
Work-in-Process
Finished Goods
Installation
Engineering in Process
Other
　　　Total Gross Inventory
Reserves
Process Payments
　　　Total Net Inventory

Figure 8-1　Inventory Budget Format

some checks and balances to insure adequate preparation of the original budget become most important. Here is a series of steps which works well:

1. A year before final budget preparation top management expresses its desires for the major goals including profits, sales, fixed capital investment and inventory. The inventory goal is expressed either as an inventory-to-sales ratio or a turnover rate for budget year-end, about two years in the future.

2. Subordinate or affiliated plants, companies and groups have three months to review these goals as applied to their operations, requesting relief in specific cases and by specific amounts. Negotiations ensue at various management levels to resolve significant differences.

3. Proposed inventory levels at year-end and in each quarter for the first one or two years are included in a one- to five-year plan submitted about four months prior to budget submittal. The numbers may or may not agree with the final data in step 2.

4. About one month prior to the beginning of the budget year, annual budgets are submitted for approval and factors negotiated during the period remaining.

5.   Final fixed budgets are prepared and adopted in the last week prior to the budget year. Flexible budgets are developed and modified during the year following agreed rules.

Peerless Topman Says . . .

"Keep performance to both fixed and flexible budgets high on your list of 'musts.' Keep them simple and review them regularly."

Group budgets become the arithmetic sum of company budgets and total corporate budgets are the sum of all groups budgets. It is better if there is no padding or adjustment at higher levels although there are frequently good arguments for some use of discretion in anticipating deviations.

Top management can initiate this rational chain of events even in corporations involving a number of groups and hundreds of companies if the principle expressed in Chapter 1 is applied to step 1. The starting point is the edict that inventory must be reduced. In all the negotiations that follow, the final result will possibly be a compromise reduction depending upon the arguments and objections presented and accepted.

The first need in measuring inventory performance against budget is to determine whether actual is above, below or at fixed budget levels. Fixed budget is the number established in the annual planning program and management must first insist on an answer to why inventories are significantly above or below this budget.

The usual reason is some other activity didn't meet its budget: Sales were off; production had problems; more material was purchased than planned anticipating shortages in supplier capacity; direct labor with the right skills couldn't be found. By far the most common explanation is that sales either were not up to plan or were above budget. This can become a catch-all excuse for all failures. Such variations should be anticipated and flexible budgets set up to show tolerable limits in related activities.

The "Flexible" Budget

A very useful approach is to make adjustments to the annual fixed budget to recognize increases or decreases in sales. Such an adjusted or *flexible* budget is a much better way to measure inventory performance. Its computation should be based on hard sales numbers, something that has actually happened, rather than on forecasts that are almost certain to be wrong.

The first attempt to "flex" a budget always suggests that fixed budgets should in some way be adjusted in relation to expected changes in future sales. This is realistic in theory since inventory is for future use. Practically, the results are likely to be unsatisfactory because of the strong human tendency to assume that delinquencies in sales-to-date will most certainly be made up by the end of the year. The more that sales-to-date fall behind budget, the more the sales-to-the-end-of-the-year are assumed to increase. This appears as a justification for the over-budget inventories created by the sales fall-down. The same sort of thinking applies to sales-to-date more than budget. Operating management is inclined to stay with the annual budget as a conservative position; this has the major advantage of requiring no explanations or excuses to corporate headquarters. Current inventory positions that look all right may actually be low.

The most incisive approach to a flexible budget is to relate that budget directly to sales-to-date. If sales-to-date are less than budget by a given percentage, the flexible inventory budget will be less than the fixed budget by the same percentage. Conversely, if sales-to-date are higher than fixed budget by a given percentage, the flexible inventory budget will be higher than the fixed budget by that same percentage.

This is simple, direct and easy to calculate. Early in the fiscal year, it can be unreasonable when relatively small differences between actual and budgeted sales are large in terms of percentages. Consider the unfortunate manager whose inventory is up at the end of the first quarter because of a relatively small fall-down in sales. The manager's flexible inventory budget is less than the fixed budget and the flexible budget has been exceeded even more than the fixed. Unreasonable though that may seem, it does call to operating management's attention early in the game the fact that inventories are going to have to be adjusted downward if sales persist in being below budget. Any operating manager who gets into the third or fourth quarter with over-budget inventories when sales are under-budget simply hasn't done his homework.

This approach to flexible budgeting puts a lot of pressure on keeping inventory in a constant relationship with sales. Without this pressure, it is easy to become complacent, resigned to the idea that inventory goes up with both sales increases and decreases. A good manager who knows how inventories compare to a target, even a moving one like a flexible budget, can use handles to get close to desired goals.

Peerless Topman Says . . .

"Be relentless in insuring fast, effective action to correct significant deviations from budgets, particularly inventory, purchased materials and direct labor."

Having lost the argument that inventory must be compared to future, not past usage, theorists are likely to make two more attempts to complicate matters. They will contend that cost of sales, not sales, is the proper output against which to measure inventory and also argue that permissable increases or required decreases should not be linear to sales but should be related to some exponential function. These people deserve an *A* for effort and compliments on their reasoning; they are quite correct—in theory. However, any possible benefits that might result from this precision will be more than offset by the added complication. If you feel generous, let them use their reasoning to explain small variances from flexible budgets.

What is really needed is a simple rule to define the measures to be used for reviewing inventory performance. The steps in such a review should be to explain that:

- Year-to-date sales are *X* percentage higher (or lower) than sales budget

- Inventory is higher (or lower) than fixed budget because . . .

- Inventory is higher (or lower) than flexible budget because . . .

By definition, everyone understands that the flexible budget is higher or lower than the fixed budget by the same X percentage.

In summary, the inventory budget is one of the most vital supports for top management's handles on inventory. Successful managers will insist that there be both fixed and flexible budgets for inventory on a month-by-month basis reflecting their objective for inventory reduction and that inventory be measured against these two budgets periodically and promptly since it has been agreed they are achievable. Really successful managers will be relentless in insuring that their organizations react promptly and effectively to correct significant variances.

Setting Inventory "Standards"

"How much inventory is enough?" Disappointing as it may be to some managers, there is no rigorous way to calculate exactly how much inventory is needed to run a business. Even if there were some sound practical way to calculate how much inventory an individual manufacturing operation needs, the number would be useless unless a company is capable of making a sound plan and operating under tight control to execute it. Don't worry about more accurate pin positioning when the bowler can't even keep the ball on the alley. In companies literally out of control, as most are, questions about the right level of inventory are purely academic in managing inventories most of the time.

Many companies, however, could determine from their formal plan how much inventory would be required if the plan could be executed. The technique is extremely simple and is available to any company with a reasonably good master production schedule and fairly complete material requirements plan. Every item controlled via material requirements planning has data on *projected available* inventory (Figure 8-2) showing the planned inventory for the item for the next three months. This is how much inventory of this item will be on hand *if the plan is met*. To get a total of all stocked items, simply sum all projected available figures for all items in the formal material requirements planning program after multiplying by the standard cost (or whatever cost is used) in evaluating inventory. This would cover stocked raw material, component and finished goods inventories.

Work-in-process could also be evaluated, however, by costing out all open manufacturing orders at the right times. For example, the planned orders in Figure 8-2 for 100 pieces scheduled to be completed in weeks 9 and 14 would be in-process in weeks 8 (month 2) and 13 (month 3). Such work-in-process could be evaluated by whatever rule is used in costing open orders. Some companies use *material only* until the order is completed, at which time the labor and overhead are added. Others apply

Part No. 316252   Ring Order Quantity = 100   Lead Time = 4 weeks   On hand = 136

Week	1	2	3	4	5	6	7	8	9	10	11	12	13	14
Requirements	26	5	32	18	2	10	3	30	21	8	14	36	6	25
On Order														
Proj. Available 136	110	105	73	55	53	43	40	10	89	81	67	31	25	100
Planned Receipt									100					100
Planned Release					100					100				

Figure 8-2   Material Requirements Plan

material plus half the labor and factory overhead as soon as the order is released and add the balance of labor and overhead when the order is completed.

Several companies are now making regular projections of inventory using this approach. The results are always interesting and quite similar. Figure 8-3 shows the type of curve obtained. Present inventories are always well above the *ideal* level which would be attained if the plan could be executed perfectly.

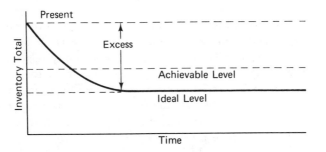

Figure 8-3   Inventory Projection

There are at least six reasons for this excess above ideal:

- Obsolete inventory with no requirements in the future
- Finished components in stock awaiting shortage items not delivered according to plan

- Shipments lower than planned because customer orders are slow in coming in

- Materials held for rework also holding up matching components and shipments

- Manufacturing overruns or purchased excesses due to commercial tolerances on quantities delivered

- Early deliveries from suppliers

Companies with this information are studying how close to the ideal plan (*achievable* in Figure 8-3) they can expect to operate. Obviously, the faster they react and the more they can get the problems under control, the closer they will be to these ideal levels. Their management is also able to determine quickly the effect of any edicts they might wish to issue relating to inventory reductions.

The ideal levels represent the minimum inventories needed to support the master plan based upon the ordering rules used to set lot-sizes and safety stocks together with any added cushions of safety time included in the plan and based also on the planned lead times. If management decides it would like to drop inventories below the ideal levels indicated, it will be necessary to change these basic ordering rules, cut lead times or drop products from the master production schedule or accomplish some of all three. The trade-off curves illustrated in Figures 2-1 and 2-2 showing return on investment data for various functions of inventories then could be used to show management the effects on operating expense, customer service and other major policy areas of significant reductions in such inventories.

Inventory theory has been available for many decades to develop such trade-off curves enabling managers to make better decisions on increasing or decreasing inventories. These trade-off curves simply relate return on investment to specific inventory changes and cannot make the decision for a manager on how much total inventory is required. The final answer on how much is wanted or needed will depend heavily on alternate needs and uses of capital. Why reduce inventories earning even a small return if the money can't be put to more productive use?

These trade-off curves add a very useful dimension to management decision-making. They change the basic questions management must answer from the old magic numbers games like, "What is the cost of carrying inventory?" and "What customer service level should we hold?", to "How much will operating costs go up if we reduce lot-size inventories?" and "What additional investment would be needed to improve customer service by five percent?" They provide a way to determine what will happen to operations if specific changes are made in inventories even if they don't help determine the total amount.

Professional inventory managers now have the tools to make a sound plan for production and inventory replenishment to meet top manage-

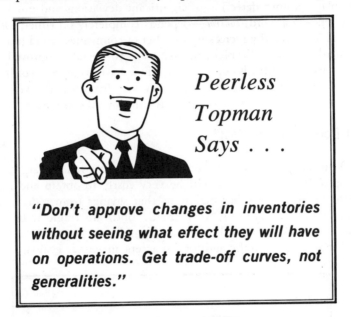

Peerless Topman Says . . .

"Don't approve changes in inventories without seeing what effect they will have on operations. Get trade-off curves, not generalities."

ment's policies and objectives and to show the effects of significant changes in plan. Making a good plan is relatively easy; it's a lot tougher to run the business, solve the problems and execute the plan. Capturing the benefits requires doing both.

The State of the Art of Record Accuracy

George Plossl is well known for his cryptic comments. With respect to record accuracy, he says in *Manufacturing Control: The Last Frontier for Profits,* "Inventory records, bills of material, manufacturing routings and standards, open order files and similar records in most companies are about as reliable as an automobile clock." For too long, inaccuracies in all of these files have been accepted as a way of life. "To err is human." "Perfection is impossible." "Learn to live with the inevitable." All of these commonly heard comments are simply "cop-outs," in the vernacular of our youth.

Philip B. Crosby, a colleague of Evert Welch's at ITT, after fighting the quality battle futilely for a long time, decided to take the stand that nothing short of perfection was really acceptable in a product to be sold to a customer. He made *Zero Defects* the password of quality control practitioners around the world. Nobody knew better than Crosby that a defect-free product depends heavily on defect-free manufacturing data. A sound plan, prompt detection of significant deviations and quick corrective action—in a word, *control*—depends completely on timely *and accurate* data. Yet a rapidly increasing number of companies spend heavily and work hard to design, implement and learn to operate improved control systems utilizing records full of errors. Few have accurate records by any standard. Few even know how sick they are. Even fewer have anything going on like a *Zero Defects* program to improve the situation.

What Does It Really Cost?

Two common beliefs explain this apathy. One holds that it is probably impossible and certainly will be very costly to obtain and maintain accurate records. The other maintains that savings from reducing errors are intangible and probably very small. Both are tragic fallacies. The out-of-pocket costs of record errors are tangible and large. The unwillingness of internal and public auditors to accept inventory evaluations based

Peerless Topman Says . . .

"Eliminate significant record errors; it saves far more than they cost. You can't make good decisions with bad data."

on inaccurate records turns loose each year in industry a monster of highly questionable worth—the traumatic *annual physical inventory.* It has value only in substantiating total inventory worth, thanks to the happy circumstance that plus and minus errors usually offset each other. It is worse than useless for correcting individual item records; *they will have more errors in them after making the adjustments indicated necessary by the annual physical inventory.*

Specific costs can be associated with errors. Staging, kitting or marshalling parts in the storeroom weeks ahead of assembling them uses unnecessary, costly space, manpower and inventory in a futile attempt to live with errors; all it really accomplishes is to make the records worse. Crash hand-counting programs to determine what's available when an important order must be shipped or a crucial decision has to be made in the plant are penalty costs. Expediting because the informal system is really in control is terribly expensive. Inventory that surfaces well after phase-out programs have been completed is a common source of high obsolescence costs. Crisis decisions and actions made necessary by bad information are always expensive. In fact, such tangible costs are not difficult to evaluate and are far in excess of the costs of eliminating errors.

A Zero Error Program

The necessary program is inexpensive, straightforward and easy to follow:

- make crystal-clear the policy that record errors must go

- define clearly the responsibility of all people setting up, up-dating, adjusting or just handling records

- provide the tools they need to meet these responsibilities

- measure accuracy levels

- find and fix the causes of errors

Like inventory, record errors will not be reduced until top management creates an atmosphere of high expectations. *The management edict is a must here as well.* Bank tellers, though paid less than most industrial workers, work in such a climate; balancing their books to the penny every day is an established, accepted way of life. We are even less tolerant of errors in other human activities. Oral polio vaccine and swine flu inoculations caused mass concern and even more massive lawsuits. People are intolerant of as low as a one-in-50-million risk when the one can be themselves or their child. No hospital manager would put up with an accident-prone nurse who had a tendency to drop babies or administer the wrong medicine, even if her error record was only one in a thousand. Why must it be assumed that office clerical and factory operating people will always make mistakes? Failure to reach perfection in record accuracy may not be fatal to the business but it guarantees chronic ills which constantly sap its strength.

Why shoot for anything less than zero errors, particularly if the cost is always less than the benefits?

People will perform as they are measured. Let people know what they are supposed to do, measure how well they do it and reward or discipline as needed. Why not apply this universal technique to recordkeeping activities? Again, a negligible cost is incurred by including record accuracy responsibilities in job descriptions and having supervisors monitor this kind of performance. Language problems, union restrictions and low pay are just more cop-outs of weak management.

Phil Crosby and his associates in Zero Defects programs established clearly the importance of an individual's knowing what is expected and having the tools to perform those expected duties. Good tools and well-documented procedures may sound to some managers like another vote for motherhood but the general lack of appreciation of the importance of good work habits and equipment is appalling. These include system tools like checking digits, hash totals, cross-checking edit routines, etc., as well as mechanical tools like counting scales, hand-held counters and nesting containers. *The locked stockroom is a must.* For small, valuable items which are tempting to thieves no one usually disagrees with the locked-stockroom concept. Strong negative reactions are generated, however, when large, heavy or fast-flowing items are involved in thievery and the economics of *point-of-use* storage are often cited to refute the need for secured stores. The fallacy is in associating walls, fences and locks with the locked-stores concept. *Physical barriers are not needed if the actual movement of materials can be locked into step with associated changes in the records* by some other means. Where they can't, however, walls and locks are mandatory. Clearly-defined control points and disciplines to insure that the system is in step with reality are vital; walls are the surest but by no means the only way to obtain this agreement. The tools needed for accurate records could be expensive but they will involve a one-time expense. Once provided, they will require little on-going maintenance. The payback will be much larger than the cost and can be realized very quickly.

Cycle counting is the procedure of verifying inventory record accuracy day-by-day, counting and checking only a sample of the total items in each period. It should replace the massive, expensive, often hysterical annual physical inventory. The advantages are obvious. The cycle count can be conducted by trained experts in an orderly manner. These may be occupied full time or may be people doing the cycle counting as only one part of their regular storekeeping, inspection, receiving or other assignments. The measurement of accuracy levels, the detection of errors and the necessary adjustments to the records proceed continuously, resulting in steady, constructive improvement in place of the disruptive, ineffective, untimely annual event. To eliminate the diminishing returns syndrome, which holds that it would cost more to eliminate small errors than it's worth, simply set a tolerance range defining significant errors. On expensive items, an error of one piece is significant; on inexpensive ones, plus or minus three percent could be tolerable and worth some extra inventory to avoid shortages. Obtained as a by product of regular duties, cycle counting costs practically nothing; even with full-time people it is still a very nominal expense.

Cycle counting is now well understood and widely practiced to verify on-hand balances in inventory records. It is just as applicable and just as effective when used to verify other records. Why not sample and check bills of material, customer orders, shop orders, purchase orders, routings and other basic records? It is possible, just as with inventory records, to get this verification at very little expense if it is done as a by-product of the daily activities of people who use or can review such records. Constant checking is the key.

The detection and correction of record errors, however, is not the principal objective of cycle counting. Its primary job must be to pinpoint the causes of errors so they can be corrected. Counting the same few items again at short intervals aids in isolating causes. These causes will be people-type problems—lost documents, poor handwriting, posting the wrong record and the like. Their elimination is a matter of training and discipline, sprucing up normal operating activities, not instituting expensive new programs. Finding and eliminating one cause improves the accuracy of many records so the approach has a multiplying effect.

False data in important records generate countless shortages; gainful improvements in processes are offset; cost-reductions in new product designs are negated, and other planned benefits are lost or unnecessarily delayed by errors in vital records. Crises and upsets incur heavy unnecessary expenses because records are wrong. The cost to industry is enormous. Accurate data alone never made a business profitable but errors can be a cancer draining its strength if allowed to persist. Their elimination contributes double benefits—immediate, in-pocket profit improvements and long-term gains through tighter control.

9

NEW SYSTEMS AND BIGGER COMPUTERS MAY BE A POOR INVESTMENT

The Role of the System

If you were to believe the bulk of the literature, the consultants, the computer manufacturers and the software houses, you would think that your company undoubtedly needs a new system. You also would be convinced that this system must include material requirements planning, statistical forecasting with tracking signals, shop floor priority lists updated daily and other wonderful techniques with odd sounding names, like *Part Period Balancing,* for determining order quantities. It is probably true that the introduction of such tools into manufacturing control activities would bring some benefits to most companies. The ancient Hawthorne experiment at Western Electric proved that any organized approach to improving operations results in some benefits. Top management should greet proposals for massive systems developments with extreme skepticism, however, challenging strongly the idea that such systems will automatically return enough in benefits to pay off their high costs.

When inventories are too high, when customer service is too low, when operations vary between organized chaos and regimented confusion and when little or nothing seems to be going according to plan, the temptation is strong to assume that a complete overhaul of the existing control system is needed. Before agreeing to this conclusion, however, top management should ask whether it is receiving the most possible out of the present system. The answer almost invariably is no. This does not mean that the present system is adequate; it simply says that most companies don't know how to run their present systems well. Why then should they assume that performance will improve sufficiently to justify a

Peerless
Topman
Says . . .

"Challenge the need for expensive, massive new systems and insist on specific payback. Be sure you're getting the best out of the present system before replacing it."

more sophisticated system and pay off its cost? Before embarking on a major system development program, it is pertinent to identify the deficiencies handicapping the present system.

In the keynote address to the 1975 International Conference of the American Production and Inventory Control Society in San Diego, George Plossl said, "Much more is required for effective manufacturing control than a sound system." He identified these additional requirements:

- a realistic master production schedule to drive the formal planning

- accurate records on which the system is based

- qualified people to operate it and to control operations with it

- an organization capable of effectively executing sound plans

Technically sound systems are necessary but they certainly are not sufficient for effective control of manufacturing. For those interested, the technical details of system design and operation are included in the Appendix; the Bibliography contains a number of references for those seeking even more information. Formal records and procedures, transaction documents to enter new information and to update data already there, notices, charts and other output reports and routine decision rules constitute the *formal system*. The primary role of this system is to provide information to people to help them make daily decisions on proper actions.

Do You Really Need a New System?

We have never yet seen a company which did not have some kind of formal system already in place. On the other hand, we have seen very few companies in which the formal system is capable of helping people control the operation. In most companies the true information on material priorities, capacity problems and other manufacturing difficulties comes from the informal system—a collection of subsystems such as hot lists, shortage reports, special hand counting and face-to-face communication among plant people in daily crisis meetings. In some cases, deficiencies in the formal system are responsible for the existence of these subsystems. In most cases, however, the formal system is not the real culprit. Too often the problems lie in poor master production schedules, inaccurate records and people who don't know how to use the system properly to help control the business or, if they do, are frustrated by in-fighting among departments. We know of no company which is getting the best possible results from its present system; the fault invariably lies in management's failure to provide the needed supporting activities.

Too much stress has been laid on developing new systems. In spite of lip service to the contrary, new systems have been made to appear as the cure for all the ills of manufacturing. Hundreds, perhaps thousands, of companies have spent huge amounts of money, time and effort in such activities. In the great majority of cases the results have been disappointing. Some have achieved real benefits but not nearly as great as were predicted. Many now have a good system but not nearly as simple and easily operated as planned. Some have solved some real problems but found more new ones raised. Some people have been helped but the great majority seem to be working harder *for the system than at their real jobs.* Expectations and promises have been high; fulfillment has left much to be desired.

The most important factors are top management attitudes and actions, a realistic master production schedule and accurate records. The lack of these foundations has contributed more to poor control than inadequate or defective systems. The system described in Figure 4-1 shows the elements needed by any manufacturing business for sound planning and control of manufacturing. You need a new system only if yours has major deficiencies when compared to this prototype. If your present system is capable of performing most of the functions indicated you will need only significant additions to fill in the gaps.

When you decide to go ahead with additions or major revisions to your system, follow these five simple rules:

- Insist on tangible cost-benefit analyses. Double the cost estimates and halve the benefits. Don't proceed if the results are marginal.

- Set a tight schedule with definite dates and specific objectives. Don't allow vague generalities. If a lot of time is needed to explore alternatives, you have the wrong people on the job.

- Use your best people full-time. Anything else is a poor risk.

- Take it a bite at a time, implementing the changes on one product line, in one department or one work center for a thorough test. Don't let your data processing experts tell you it can't be done this way; it can and is far less risky.

- Review progress regularly and often. Don't tolerate delays. If it's really worth doing, it should be done now.

It is certain that your real problems will be in improving the major support activities: master production scheduling, record accuracy and enough qualified people to operate a system effectively. Don't start a major systems improvement program without first investigating thoroughly these three vital areas. Many companies are working hard developing new systems. Those few will succeed who spend at least as much money and time on these supporting activities as on the system itself.

The First Rule of System Improvement

To be successful, any system improvement of significant size must be managed throughout its duration by someone from the group who will be its prime user. If the principal user is not involved in, and in fact in charge of, any new or changed system development, forget it! If the principal user is too busy and cannot be spared for the improvement effort, postpone it until that person can be available. The principal user is the person who will head the department when the improvement is installed. This rule not only presages doom for consultant-managed design and implementation programs, it also implies pessimism about programs managed by in-house staff, systems or data processing personnel. There has been no greater source of misdirected, ill-fated and futile efforts than the well-intended work performed by such people. This is not to criticize their capabilities. Another great waste is bringing in someone other than the principal user, who can be described as a "user type," in the hopes that this type of person will serve the purpose. The fact that an individual is not an employee of the system or data processing departments is not qualification for filling the principal user role.

Peerless Topman Says . . .

"Give the principal user the assignment of developing a new system and the sole responsibility for making it work."

Prior to retirement, Evert Welch engineered a series of seminars jointly managed by his staff at ITT and individuals from IBM. The theme was the importance of user participation in the development of control systems and system changes with emphasis on just how one succeeds in living with electronic data processing. The seminars were unique in a number of respects:

● The audience at the seminars was limited to ITT manufacturing personnel, in other words, *users only*. Systems and data processing personnel were excluded intentionally so that the sessions could be devoted exclusively to those line individuals who were to be served by the system and were directly affected by changes.

● The same exclusion was applied to the discussion leaders. IBM arranged for operating managers to replace the usual talented but sales-minded professional educators for whom they are so well and favorably known. ITT did the same and all their speakers were manufacturing executives.

- The presentations were actual case studies of planning for new systems or major changes with open discussion of the resulting successes and failures. In particular, the importance of the role of the user was emphasized. Operating personnel, given an opportunity to describe their problems, were frank and open in recognizing the need for their active roles in such projects.

- The usual discussion at such seminars of the state of the art of data processing hardware and software was not allowed. Discussion about computers was limited to the basic problems of living with mechanized data processing. Great importance was attached to record accuracy and George Plossl's film on that subject from the IBM series of material requirements planning had a prominant spot on the agenda of all meetings.

- Discussion of technical details of systems and techniques was limited to what actually happened in a particular case study. The general feeling was that making systems and techniques work for the user was more important than the details of system design or techniques chosen.

- Modular approaches were highlighted. One of the best case studies was that of an ITT company which had a project with only one objective, to clean up the bills-of-material once and for all.

- An Italian production control manager stole one show with his description of a successful operating system installation that seemed to defy all of the "sacred cows" of manufacturing control systems. It started with a combination of material requirements planning and reorder points that would seem to most to be incompatible. The part numbering system was unconventional, as was the structure of the bills-of-material. Order and safety stock rules were eminently simple and sound but hardly in accord with current statistical thinking. Exception reporting was the prime objective with more than usual reliance on the computer to supply information only as it was needed for taking action. The innovation of never printing out a complete stock status report was typical. In retrospect, the reasons for the success of the system are clear; the numbers that came out of the computer had such a high degree of credibility that they were accepted and used by all and, since operating management helped with the design of the system, they understood it thoroughly.

- In the seminars, time for discussion, for the most part, was unlimited. Things that didn't get settled in the daytime came in for a thorough rehash in the late hours of the evening.

- Several of these seminars were presented across the United States and one in Great Britain. Each was a challenge because each had a new group of leaders from both ITT and IBM who had to be indoctrinated into the specific restrictions. It took a bit of doing; there was always some speaker who wanted to give in to an urge to make a pitch for a favorite control system or hardware but who wasn't allowed to do so. In the end, it worked out well, IBM paid ITT the compliment of including a variation on the theme in its own educational series.

Evert Welch retired before he could fully accomplish his goal of terminating all control system change projects not managed by the principal user.

However, his staff was successful in instituting strong regulations requiring the participation of key users in the management of new projects. Every project for a new system or a major system change coming under the cognizance of ITT headquarters requires user *sign off*. Top management at ITT takes a strong position on mandatory user participation in control system projects. A regular program of interviews with these users now assures their understanding of and participation in the project. One significant benefit was that after-the-fact approvals of upgraded computers ceased quickly when some unneeded installations were returned to the manufacturer.

System Documentation

More good systems have been misused and even discarded because of lack of good documentation than is generally recognized. Failure to provide an adequate written description of a system and how it is used is one of the most harmful of the false economies practiced in management. Like the weather, good documentation is something about which everyone talks but no one does anything. If a system is written up at all, the job is done at the end of the development program by people who would sooner get on with more interesting work. Little if any effort is devoted subsequently to recording the changes and new developments to keep the writeup current and complete.

Two types of documentation are needed: first, a detailed system description including flow charts and computer programming for the use of data processing people who will be modifying it in the future, and second, *a generalized description for the system users in business English* telling what the system is supposed to do, how it does its job, what it needs to keep functioning and what the output reports really say. Data processing people characteristically do a much better job on the first type because they expect to need and really do use the material developed. If user documentation is prepared at all, it is usually written by systems people who have great difficulty writing business English, do not expect to use it themselves and are unfamiliar with the users' true needs and interests.

The price paid for lack of good documentation is very high. First, a fine opportunity is missed for inexpensive education and development of qualified system users. The best way to be sure they really understand the system and how it functions is to have them write up a description, spell out the system's needs and explain how they will use its outputs. This is the best method for user training and development.

A second major cost of poor documentation is the price paid in false starts and wasted efforts in improving the system or developing major modifications. If the documentation is weak or lacking and if those who developed the original design are no longer with the company, a good system may have to be discarded. A new system is too high and unnecessary an expense to pay for this failure.

Third, lack of documentation makes familiarizing new people with their jobs unnecessarily time-consuming and uncertain, leading to costly mistakes. A fourth major cost, and probably the most important, is failure to use the system to its best advantage. People who are not familiar with how the system really functions will not understand when and how to apply their own judgment which is so necessary to compensate for the limitations of the system and the data it provides. Inevitably they will either follow the system blindly or set up their own alternative subsystems, both equally disastrous alternatives.

It would be very worthwhile to document present systems if no documentation now exists for the users. We don't mean to cover office walls and fill volumes of books with flow charts, samples of forms and system jargon. What is needed is a simple narrative description (playscript style is very effective) clarifying interactions between people and the system. It is far more important that the material be organized in logical fashion, be complete and have a good index than to have it written in elegant prose.

The only really valid test for good documentation is whether or not it is used. Make it too elaborate, too difficult to find information needed, make only a very few copies and keep them hidden away carefully in a desk drawer or bookcase and you will guarantee that documentation will not be kept up to date. A dog-eared, well-thumbed, brief and handy writeup on everyone's desk with plenty of handwritten marginal notes is preferred. This is good user documentation. The more complex your systems become, the more your people need this kind of help. It's as unpopular and unglamorous as regular exercise but it's necessary for good company health.

The Computer—Help or Hindrance?

Whether you like it or not, the computer is a vital part of manufacturing control systems and it's here to stay. Many of us have had unpleasant and downright maddening experiences with computers in banks, airlines, hotels and credit card agencies. Like Bernard Levin said in one of his columns in the London Daily Mail, "I begin to believe that the computer is not the great god we have been led to believe, but a hollow idol, manipulated by crafty priests." Some managers still think they can get along without it but then many people still refuse to fly in airplanes and some will not even use the telephone. You can get along without modern tools but your business will suffer.

Parkinson's first law was never more appropriate than in computer applications. Unused computer capacity is considered by the data processing "wizards" as a black mark on their record and a challenge to their ingenuity and salesmanship. They can be counted on to search around for something to fill this open capacity, some new program that someone would like and believes, even erroneously, might be helpful.

Does this sound familiar? Because of the pressures of installing such new programs, there is usually not enough time to review existing ones to find out which are no longer being used. Then along comes a program with real payback—like an improved manufacturing control system—that needs lots of time on the computer. But now there is not enough capacity available and consideration must be given to a larger machine. This is timely since the present hardware is really out of date and should be replaced with the latest-generation equipment.

Conversion of all the existing programs to the new hardware, of course, will save considerable computer processing costs for some lucky users but will take many months. Meanwhile the new control system obviously cannot be started until this vital work is done. Such delay is truly unfortunate but it can't be helped. The job could be done more quickly, of course, if more systems and programming staff were added.

When the new programs are finally completed, they will be run in proper priority with all the other work being done by the now-massive data processing installation. Financial reports at the close of the accounting periods will always be given preference over operating data because "it's their machine" and the scorekeepers need the information; the players can wait. It probably will be suggested that service to the players could be much better wtih a bigger machine and more staff and the ponderous, expensive cycle will start again.

This may sound like tongue-in-cheek satire to some. Many managers today, however, are asking themselves whether or not large, central, data processing installations are really worth the cost. More top managers are becoming frustrated at the high expense, low benefits and seemingly endless delays and are struggling to find a better solution. One does exist.

The Way to Effective Computer Use

The way out begins with a reappraisal of the primary roles of your data processing staffs and system users. Since computers are here to stay, you obviously will continue to need the experts who:

- thoroughly understand the hardware and software

- can bring some order out of the chaos of a multitude of programming languages

- know how to set up and maintain a common data base so that anyone writing programs to provide access to information on customer orders, bills of material, process routings and standards, inventory balances, cost information and other basic data knows where to find it in the system files

- can establish standards for system project plans and documentation

- can audit systems and procedures at intervals to see that these standards are maintained

You will always need such experts. But ask yourself, "Why should they actually process the data?" Is it really necessary that the computer experts run the computers? The manufacturing engineering experts don't

Peerless Topman Says . . .

"Treat manufacturing control systems and their computers exactly like productive machinery and process equipment."

run the sophisticated production machines or process equipment. The failure to see clearly that control systems and data processing equipment are essentially no different from complex manufacturing machinery has led us down the garden path to bigger, but not better, data processing installations doing more numerous, but less productive, data processing tasks.

A few companies now assign the prime responsibility for sound systems working effectively to those line operating managers responsible for control of manufacturing costs and inventories. Their responsibility includes recognizing their need for new control systems, designing and installing them and operating them effectively. Recent developments in computer technology and pricing make it possible to let them have and run their own computers. Data base management techniques now provide open-ended files which can be altered or expanded as the needs of the business require, without major alterations to existing programs using these files.

Mini- and micro-computers are now priced low enough to be the economical way to provide on-site hardware and software so manufacturing files and control systems are clearly the property and responsibility of the users. This ends all the buck-passing to that nebulous "data processing bunch in the corporate headquarters." A network of small machines can be placed throughout manufacturing operations, run on identical programs and maintain common files which can be accessed by other computers to collect control information for higher levels of management. A hierarchy of machines thus supports the control needs of a hierarchy of managers.

The advantages gained are tremendous. Among them are:

- the total hardware investment is considerably lower

- computer hardware real (not on-line) utilization is greatly increased

- the time required to implement new programs or extended programs into new areas is shortened considerably

- the responsibility for getting programs going and making them pay off clearly belongs to operating people, not central data processing

- the ability of systems to serve users and be more responsive to their needs is greatly improved

- the payback is surer and comes sooner

The direction of the future is clear. Significant progress already has been made in many companies. The greatest impediment to more rapid development along these lines is the existence of massive, central, corporate data processing installations and staffs. Like any government bureaucracy these people can always find supporters and justification for their existence and can present convincing arguments that no other approach will possibly work. Most of these people sincerely believe they are right. As with the massive failure of the U. S. Postal Service, however, the intertia, frustration and economic loss of present computer installations are the most compelling reasons why a better way must be found. The job will have to be done sooner or later. The real question is why wasn't it started long ago when the need became obvious and the right way clear? With proper use of computers and their supporting staffs, top management can change a wasteful, suffocating burden into a vital, productive asset.

10

PROFESSIONALISM IN MANUFACTURING CONTROL

To insure successful control of inventories and manufacturing, top management must be certain that the key people involved are professionals in the fullest sense of the word. A professional in any field is one who is thoroughly familiar with the body of knowledge in that field, understands its language, knows its techniques—their strengths and weaknesses—and has had experience in applying these techniques successfully. Furthermore, to merit the designation of professional, broad experience and full qualifications are necessary, as well as a dedication to fulfilling assigned responsibilities by seeking to perform to the highest personal and company standards. A professional is not a beginner; he has more to offer than good intentions. Nor is the professional simply engaged in business on a temporary basis in a holding pattern awaiting opportunities in some other preferred field.

The professional excells in three areas of competence:

- Ethics

- Knowledge

- Capability

Ethics

As long as there have been professions the matter of members' ethics has been of concern. Many codes have been written to define standards of personal and business morality. To date, no such code has been developed

109

in the field of manufacturing control although it is now recognized clearly as a profession. Scattered attempts have been made in the area of purchasing where gifts and gratuities are an ever-present problem and opportunities for improper disclosure abound.

Peerless
Topman
Says . . .

"Get real pros running your manufacturing control systems. You can't afford amateurs."

In the 1970s, a series of occurrences brought renewed emphasis to this important factor of personal behavior. Widespread revelations of the breakdown of morals among people in government culminated in the resignations of the country's President and Vice President and numerous other public figures at national, state and local levels. Actions previously accepted, at least tacitly, became matters of great concern and brought the wrath and ire of the public. No one can even estimate the costs and damage of these past misconducts in government.

It is impossible also to evaluate the losses that business has sustained as a result of employee dishonesty, loose morality and poor ethics. Outright thievery, like the hand in the petty cash drawer, deserves little more than passing comment; the misappropriation of another's money or property, whether a person or a corporation, is clearly unacceptable everywhere. The acceptance of bribes in many forms, also revealed in the '70s to have been widespread in business internationally, is not so black and white; it has many shades of gray. The practice of entertaining and giving business associates gratuities and holiday gifts has had broad acceptance. Is it the real intent of the giver to influence the decisions of the receiver to the possible detriment of the latter's company? Does the giver consider the customer as fair game or are the actions believed to be an acceptable form of advertising? These are difficult questions which permit people to rationalize their actions, whatever their true motives may be. To the true professional, the acceptance of any such gifts is comparable to the hand in the till; there is no answer except *zero tolerance* in such matters when there is any possibility of unwarranted influence intended or implied.

A more subtle and less discussed violation of honesty and ethics in business is the failure to disclose unpleasant facts to management. Instead the tendency is to tell only what management really likes to hear. Every boss wants to be told that things are fine, or, if they aren't, the situation's under control and better days are just around the corner. The practice of sorting good news from bad and not passing along the bad is so prevalent that management levels are often referred to as *filters,* often so diluting and distorting the facts that little truth actually reaches the top. The fact that many businesses survive under these conditions speaks well for top management systems of espionage but there is no doubt that management could be more effective if there were full disclosure of all facts—pleasant and unpleasant.

Ethics, honesty and integrity demand a high standard for the communication of information, especially upwards. With teenage shoplifting

Peerless Topman Says . . .

"Insist your managers tell the truth and the whole truth. What you don't know can hurt you."

considered by do-gooders as simply a phase of growing up, concerned retailers have used television warnings that, "No ifs, ands or buts, shoplifting is a crime!" Let us paraphrase that for business purposes: *"No ifs, ands or buts, misinforming the boss is dishonest and a violation of one's integrity and ethics."*

"It might still work out all right if things break for us" is a companion phrase to "Don't tell the boss because he will be unhappy." This easily leads to the tongue-in-cheek promise that "We will complete the order and deliver as requested." Too often the delivery is missed but the customer is already locked in to the date and will have to bow to the inevitable and accept any reasonable way out. The real cost comes in the customer's future attitude.

It's very human to hope that something will happen to soften the consequences of failure but the normal result is generally only a temporary reprieve. The most tragic case in our experience involved a colleague of Evert Welch's during the Korean War period. It all started with a series of innocent looking errors in judgment that went unreported to management. They snowballed into a cumulative loss to the company of more than $1 million. A coverup was attempted and its failure resulted in a suicide.

It all started with a "quickie" design of a complex device during wartime. Certain electronic components in final assembly could not be precisely specified but were indicated to be "chosen as required." In effect, these components were used like adjusting screws to compensate for various tolerance pileups in the circuitry. It might be called shabby design but it seemed justified by the urgent need for large quantities of the device.

No added potential costs in excess components of this "select and fit" process were built into the original cost estimates. The assumption was made that the electronic characteristics of the components used would stabilize early in the program into some sort of a reasonably forecastable statistical pattern of usage. There is no doubt that such cost adjustments could have been negotiated at any time during the early production on full disclosure of the situation to management and the customer.

Large volumes of components were required. The required component characteristics would stabilize for short periods, then change abruptly again. Each time this happened, the hope was that the next gyration would use up inventory excesses from past orders. It was further anticipated that follow-on orders would accomplish the same purpose. In the end, the contracts were completed leaving masses of components costing about a million dollars unused in inventory and not properly reflected in product costs. Even at that point two possible alternative actions still existed. One was full disclosure: tell management that a long series of poor order decisions had been made and explain why this information had been withheld; the other was to take a chance that future contracts for other devices might use up the excess inventory. In the hope of a miracle, the coverup was planned and middle managers directly involved agreed to it.

The miracle didn't happen. Real requirements for the inventory did not develop, the overage came to light and most of those involved began establishing their individual alibis. In the end, it was the production control manager who was discredited and demoted, though not actually discharged. After a few weeks of living with the memory, he took his life.

There is no place in key roles in business for nonprofessional managers whose honesty and integrity are questionable.

A Word about Ethics in Purchasing

Distasteful as it may be, you can't talk about the procurement function and the relations between buyer and seller without at least a few words about ethics. As this is written, this country is going through a sort of "new morality" in government and business which has made the receipt by public servants of gratuities, however small, unacceptable.

Industry has had its share of Watergates. The temptation to accept a few bottles of liquor, a paid vacation, or a new set of tires is strong. No buyer worth his salt would ever admit to having been influenced by such actions from a vendor. No vendor would agree that gifts and courtesies are actually bribes. Specific rules attempting to define what can and cannot be accepted haven't been effective in government or industry and probably never will be. The only answer that works is to refuse *any* and *every* gratuity. That means no pencils, no memo pads, no calendars, zilch, zero, nada! Only in the atmosphere of zero tolerance on gratuities, coupled with professional dealings on priority and capacity can the buyer and seller achieve this mutual respect that is so important to business.

Knowledge

Peter Drucker pointed to a real need in his book, *Manufacturing*. Rather than increase productivity of manual workers, the basic need is to develop knowledgeable workers. The knowledgeable professional in manufacturing control has had enough years of actual on-the-job experience to fully develop and test his or her ability to cope with the many problems that are presented. As in all other professions, however, formal education is an important part of knowledgeability in manufacturing control. There are always exceptional individuals coming up through the ranks who can earn their stripes with a minimum of formal education in any field. It can be done also in manufacturing control and such people have to be given careful consideration when management personnel are chosen. Conversely, there are professional theorists who live in a world of ideas without ever coming to grips with reality. One proves that a high level of academic achievement is not necessary to success in this field; the other proves that education alone is no guarantee of success.

The well-educated inventory control manager has the same advantage that the college graduate has in engineering. Although a fairly recent development, both Industrial Engineering and Business Administration schools now offer courses covering the fundamental principles of manufacturing control. Both teach the orderly approach necessary to the solution of problems met by today's business managers. Technical societies, trade associations, computer manufacturers, software houses and consultants also offer courses, seminars and workshops on material relevant to the field.

The American Production and Inventory Control Society (APICS)

Participation in the activities of this society is an absolute must for the professional in manufacturing control and will be extremely useful to anyone working in or close to this field. APICS was formed in Cleveland in 1957 by a handful of dedicated individuals who recognize the need for a professional organization for the exchange of ideas and experiences in what was then called "Production and Inventory Control." In no way could they have visualized the growth and contribution of this organization in the next two decades. In this period the society spread worldwide with active membership over twenty thousand in just twenty years.

Local chapters are now active in large cities in practically every state in the U. S., in Canada, in several European countries and in many developed countries in South America and Africa. The great bulk of people in manufacturing industry are within practical travel distance of some worthwhile APICS activity. These include monthly chapter meetings featuring speakers of local and national reputation, periodic conferences, training courses, seminars and workshops. The society's primary goal is education of its members.

The annual international conference has become the high point of APICS's activities. In 1976 sessions in Atlanta, Georgia, discussing 90 subjects in 12 major classifications attracted an audience well in excess of 2,000 from many countries. Like each of its predecessors, this conference broke all records for attendance, scope and interest.

Indicating the breadth of interest, the 12 main themes were:

Plan and execution

Relationship to the bottom line

Inventory management

Master production scheduling

Manufacturing systems

Forecasting and capacity control

Productivity gains

Record accuracy

Material requirements planning

Professionalism

System design and implementation

Warehousing and distribution

In addition to the conference sessions there were 20 special industry presentations, mostly related to data processing, presenting advanced approaches to control system design and operation.

APICS Certification

The Society has developed its own certification program. Since 1974 it has provided examinations so members and others can test their knowledge of the field. Administered by the nation's largest and most professional organization specializing in the management of testing programs, APICS now offers examinations leading to *"Certified Practitioner"* and *"Fellow"* rankings depending on the grade attained. The tests are given on five topics twice a year:

Inventory planning

Shop floor control

Forecasting

Capacity planning and control

Material requirements planning

The program was developed to meet three objectives: to define better the body of knowledge in the field, to provide means whereby an individual could be measured for comprehension of principles, techniques and their application to the problems of industry, and to help close the gap between academia and the Society's activities. Significant success has been achieved in all three.

George W. Plossl was National Chairman of this effort in its first four years and W. Evert Welch served on the Capacity Planning and Control Committee. We can attest to the importance of the program to both the society and industry. Achieving "Certification" is now recognized in this field as the badge of the professional. More companies every day are making it a requirement that individuals in key jobs hold this rank. Some pay bonuses to those achieving it. Earning the degree of "Fellow" is to attain the highest honor of the society.

Capability

Given a fund of knowledge and the will to use it with honesty and integrity, professionalism also involves capability, the execution of the requirements of a position to the satisfaction of top management. In this field it requires both education and experience, having met and solved the practical operating problems before. It is measured by on-the-job results.

Since manufacturing control involves so many shared responsibilities—forecasting, master scheduling, systems development, etc.—and interactions with other departments, success will require respect by peers, communication skills and the courage to support unpopular views. Since most of the important decisions involve compromises, it is no activity for anyone interested in being popular with associates. Usually the best that can be expected is no criticism. The rewards come from making a real contribution to company success. The potential of improved manufacturing control is enormous in helping almost every company to give better service to customers while earning more profit with less investment.

Well-educated, experienced, management-oriented professionals in manufacturing control are taking their places in the ranks of outstanding management. Require your personnel to be real pros in this field and help them achieve it.

The Use of Qualified Consulting Services

The development of internal professionalism and competence can be greatly enhanced by the use of well-chosen outsiders. The use of outside consultants in many specialty fields is well-accepted in modern industry. Manufacturing control is no exception. Outsiders can provide objectivity, specialized knowledge, broad experience and added additional arms and legs to an improvement effort. They can improve communication among the various organization levels in your business and even point out and help make top management decisions that inside people would hesitate to suggest.

Education Vs. Implementation

Consultants "come in two flavors," so to speak. Some specialize in *implementation* and usually feature a stable of bright young people armed with procedure manuals who work to create a new system for the client embodying modern techniques. A senior member of his own firm directs the operation. The approach is common but it's expensive by any measure of comparison and its failure rate is high. All too often, the consultant's understanding of the business is superficial and the benefits provided are

Peerless Topman Says . . .

"Don't be above using the services of out-siders. The right kind can be helpful."

far outweighed by their failure to develop company personnel properly. All too often such consultants did some good work once in a company which employed them but are now "floaters," moving from job to job and from one consulting firm to another, offering more in the way of available man-hours than in effectiveness. For the company that really knows what it wants but needs bodies to get it, such people can be useful.

The other school of consultants furnish *advice, counsel* and *education,* leaving the actual work of design and implementation to in-house person-nel. Generally describing themselves as *counselors* rather than *consultants,* this group subscribes to an axiom that the authors feel is the first rule of successful improvement implementation—"If you want the muscles, you'll have to do the exercises." Such counselors command high daily fees but spend little total time with the client. Their success rate is high.

The Function of the Counselor

The counselor provides an invaluable link between the principal user of systems and the best of modern practices as the counselor has observed them in other companies in comparable circumstances. This evaluation of what, in fact, is comparable requires that familiarity with the business at hand and management's goals for its improvement be developed. This, together with diagnosing the major control deficiencies, requires a maximum of one week.

Services can be rendered to the client in a number of different ways. The first is including client personnel in scheduled training courses open to people from other companies so that they can be exposed to the experiences of their peers while getting up to speed on the state of the art, principles and techniques. This offering of public training courses is characteristic of the counselors.

The second service is providing in-plant training programs so that a number of user personnel can be taught modern concepts in their own terminology related to their particular situation and adapted to their current needs.

The third is the most important function—making periodic reviews of proposed plans, evaluating progress in implementing them and exposing delays and bottlenecks that have appeared since a previous visit.

Ernie Theisen, while a colleague of George Plossl's, summarized the case for consultants very well when he wrote, "Your main purpose for calling in a consultant should be to use his knowledge and experience to assist you in improving your system so that corporate objectives can be met with optimum efficiency. Any other reason is a waste of his time and your money."

11

INSIST YOUR ORGANIZATION EXECUTE THE PLAN

Formal System Behavior

"Our society has largely evolved by a process of chance mutation and adaptation, in the unplanned manner of natural selection. It reacts to major problems only when they starkly present themselves." This quotation from *The Computerized Society* by James Martin and Adrian R. D. Norman aptly describes the way most manufacturing is controlled. All companies have formal plans for operations supposed to help them maintain control. Few, however, operate in a *planning mode*.

For many years it has been general practice for manufacturing people to ignore the formal system and work around it and in spite of it through the use of their own informal subsystems—short sheets, black books, hot lists and other patchwork approaches—reacting to today's crises. This hasn't been due to obstinacy just for the sake of being obstinate; it was the only practical way to get the information they really needed. Every company has a formal system. However, in most companies even today it is the informal subsystems which people need and use to control manufacturing.

The immediate objective must be to make the formal system capable of helping people plan and control and also to make the system itself easier to control. Until now, ease of control has not been a primary objective of systems designers developing manufacturing control systems. Rather, the emphasis has been on providing a complete, soundly-conceived system able to create the original plan quickly and to replan it frequently and in depth. *This emphasis on the ability to replan is now seen as the primary cause of many failures to control.*

The modern manufacturing plant consists of a multitude of produc-

Peerless Topman Says . . .

"Don't put much faith in replanning systems. Insist that your people execute the plan, not just revise it."

tive facilities—machines, equipment, assembly stations, packaging lines, etc. Hundreds or thousands of raw materials and component parts flow through these facilities into a wide variety of end products shipped to a large number of customers. The number of different paths that can be followed through this maze is often beyond comprehension. The management of these flows to achieve the desired end-product outputs is a problem in logistics much more complex than air traffic control in a busy airport during a thunderstorm.

The initial objective of formal control systems is to simulate the flow of materials through the available processing facilities, using predetermined ordering and scheduling rules and average lead times. With the aid of modern computers, this simulation produces specific recommendations on what is needed when based on optimum, or near optimum, planning. Furthermore, computers make it possible to replan frequently and to identify detailed changes from the previous plan, thus generating a list of new actions needed to meet the latest conditions. This replanning can be done on a *regenerative,* or periodic, basis often weekly, rerunning the entire simulation to produce a new plan in its entirety.

Promising as all of this seems, the fact remains that most such applications to date have been unsuccessful. A prime cause has been that the number of suggested changes at each replanning has been so large that people are unable to cope with all of them. Since the number of items on the list relates to the time period between replannings, the first attempt to solve the problem has been to increase the frequency of replanning. At the extreme, it may be done on a continuous, *real-time* basis processing new inputs via *net change* to indicate not only changes from the preceding plan but also sending out a constant stream of signals. It takes very little thought to realize this will generate at least as many changes as the periodic approach; usually more notices come out, some reversing previous notices. This is literally a massive assault on the symptoms and, unfortunately, usually aggravates the disease—*too many sources of change*, including dynamic techniques in the system and poor execution of the original plan.

It is an unfortunate characteristic of all rigorous mathematical approaches that a highly precise answer is easier to obtain than one that is practical and useful. The Economic Order Quantity formula is a case in point. It has the ability to indicate that an order quantity of 1,587 is *better* than 1,586 or 1,588 based on the factors considered in the formula. It is difficult to build into the formula the fact that 1,600 or even 1,000 or 2,000 is a much more desirable answer when all relevant factors are considered. The material requirements planning algorithm has the same general characteristic. By rigorous and straightforward calculations it is possible to produce a list of *every* change that results from the last replanning. It is much more difficult to recognize those changes that are really important and to eliminate or suppress those that are not.

Stability Is the Key

Improving the stability of the system itself produces the best results, rather than finding ways to dampen its output. It is becoming more and more apparent that changes to improve stability may be more productive than refinements and enhancements to the control system. Unfortunately, most of the improvements along this line have evolved from necessity rather than from plan. A good example of this evolution is the Master Production Schedule. The volume of paperwork generated when you try to include all specific end products, intermediates and replacement parts in a Master Production Schedule has dictated the development of such schedules for more appropriate lower-level *modules* or bulk products. The result of improving the definition of what is scheduled is more stable output from the formal plan that is more practical and easier to manage. Chapter 6 discusses this important *handle* on the business in detail and stresses the need for stabilizing such schedules and forbidding tinkering.

The same wasteful, useless output occurs when dynamic adjustments are made in order quantities, safety stocks, lead times or other parameters in the formal planning programs. Pseudo-sophistication in such techniques is hamstringing good management of sound programs. The system is highly precise but the environment is not.

End-item requirements of long lead-time items on a period-to-period basis far into the future are subject to constant change. The ability to make frequent changes to match *planned replenishment orders* exactly to these requirements was once hailed as one of the great breakthroughs for material requirements planning and computerized controls. Unhappy experience has shown that the resulting rescheduling of lower level parts or assemblies already in process has made it necessary to designate certain planned orders as *firm planned orders*, not to be adjusted by the computer without human intervention.

Another of the computerized material requirements planning-based program's apparent strong points has been its ability to recompute batch quantities to match changing requirements. *Dynamic order quantities,* once considered a real benefit of mechanized order systems, are now found to be more trouble than they are worth in most applications. Safety stocks, long considered a necessity to live in a world of uncertainty, can be set by rigorous mathematical analysis. It's now clear they are a snare and a delusion, distorting the most vital information needed from the formal systems—*when* you really need the item—and causing unnecessary nervousness in the system when they are recalculated regularly.

Reorder point techniques, once the whipping boy of the material requirements planning purists, are now handled as *time-phased order points,* where the best forecasts available are in terms of averages and variabilities. As systems are further simplified and stabilized, the use of conventional reorder point techniques will return to favor in many applications. All these techniques are discussed in detail in the Appendix.

While most practitioners are still concentrating on faster ways to detect and reflect more deviations from plan and to replan even more frequently, it is now evident that the real payoff can come only from an orderly approach to simplifying and stabilizing systems. Certainly, the causes of unnecessary nervousness should be eliminated. All of the modifications discussed here have been for the purpose of making the original planning relevant for a longer period of time. The advantages seem obvious. If you have output schedules you don't have to change, if you have planned orders that don't move as to due date, if you have order quantities that aren't unstable, if you have fixed safety stocks in limited application, your whole environment is more controllable and manageable. It is commendable to be able to identify needed changes specifically and quickly, but it is more useful to avoid alterations to the plan when the confusion, distraction and cost exceed the benefits. *The real benefits come from the execution of a sound, simple plan, not replanning.*

The Impact of Organization Forms

There is no such thing as one best form of organization and the company that constantly seeks to solve its problems through organizational change is a company that will continue to be in trouble. A good example of almost fanatical dedication to an organizational idea is Materials Management, a concept that became popular in the 1950s and has had many strong proponents as well as detractors ever since. Its purpose was to bring under one manager the various functions dealing with materials and their flow through the plant. It was supposed to resolve differences in philosophy, objectives and priorities between Material Control and Purchasing Departments, each vying for the major share of responsibility in the materials picture. Its greatest weakness was the focus on materials, ignoring machinery, manpower and money which are equally important in manufacturing. It has failed more often than not because it tried to establish a referee rather than concentrating on developing teamwork to solve the real problems of lack of sound systems, record errors and unqualified people in key roles. Where it has succeeded, its contribution has been really only improved coordination and communications among

Peerless
Topman
Says . . .

"Identify clearly the primary responsibility of each organizational group and measure how well it meets it."

groups already clear on their roles and equipped with the necessary system using sound data and qualified people to run it.

There is no best form or organization and there are no clean lines of unique responsibility in controlling manufacturing. Many important tasks must be shared. There are primary responsibilities, however, which should be clearly defined and understood. Peter Drucker in *Management* said, "The purpose of an organization is to make the strengths of people productive and their weaknesses irrelevant." Success will come only when a team of individuals works together toward a common, defined and measurable goal.

Departmental Responsibilities

It is widely believed that the primary responsibility of Engineering is to *invent* saleable products in accordance with management's plan for the proliferation of the product line. Invention for its own sake is great fun but this kind belongs in Research Departments, not in Engineering. Having invented something practical, an integral part of the primary responsibility of Engineering is to develop their inventions into products that can be manufactured profitably and to continue to improve the products throughout their economic lives. *Equally integral is the responsibility for telling others what the product is* through drawings, specifications and bills of material produced in a language and a format that Manufacturing, Marketing, Finance and others can use. Of particular importance is the bill of materials. Engineering views this as their last duty, and an onerous one. To those who use it—nearly everyone does—it is their starting information. It's the structure on which the formal manufacturing plan hangs. Allowing Engineering to shirk this part of its primary responsibility places undue burdens on others and handicaps control.

Marketing's primary responsibility is to provide intelligence on the needs of the marketplace, forecasting potential salability of new and existing products. It must provide also an objective evaluation of customer reactions to the company's products and services. Marketing has a major role in all forecasting reviews and revisions, as well as in setting priorities among customers and between customer orders when the realities of production show that the needs of all cannot be met. Theirs is not just the job of getting orders: *They have a vital role in planning and control activities, helping make the hard choices among the limited alternatives.*

The job of manufacturing control is to develop and operate the formal manufacturing control system that provides information on the needed resources of materials, manpower, machinery and money. This must include the responsibility for the way data is gathered and processed; this cannot be relinquished to specialized systems or computer services groups. *They are solely responsible for the selection and application of control techniques used in their systems and for timely detection and reporting of significant deviations from plan.*

Manufacturing's primary responsibility is *to utilize people, machines and materials effectively and economically* to produce the planned total of the right products and to participate actively in the formulation and revision of operating plans.

Purchasing's primary responsibility is *to develop reliable sources and to negotiate prices for materials and services* required. It must evaluate alternate materials and competitive vendors, making price an important part but not the sole consideration in that evaluation.

It is the primary responsibility of Data Processing and Systems *to provide expert staff services to all other departments* of the company. These include the development of common data bases, the avoidance of redundant files, advice, counsel, education and assistance to their user departments in the technical capabilities of data processing hardware and software. They must abandon "computereze" and jargon for business English. Whether or not they operate the hardware, the responsibility for effective systems lies with the line managers in user departments.

Good Execution Requires Responsibilities Shared Effectively

The principal decisions of manufacturing control practically always affect more than one department. Much has been written about the con-

Peerless
Topman
Says . . .

"Clarify shared responsibilities and demand teamwork among managers in meeting them."

flicting goals of Manufacturing, Marketing, Finance and Engineering. Each is pictured—and it is all too often true—as having tunnel vision, or seeing only its own selfish aims. Ordering techniques are portrayed as resolving these difficulties by allowing Finance to evaluate inventory costs, Marketing to set up acceptable customer service levels and Manufacturing to identify operating costs. The presumption is that the ordering technique will produce the optimum compromise among these conflicting goals and all will be well. But, all rarely turns out well! It is very clear that even the best techniques are all too often impotent; blind reliance on formulas is the worst sort of misplaced faith.

Sound systems will be nonproductive without active and amicable cooperation among the major departments. Many companies operate as if the department heads were natural enemies. We have suggested that these companies adopt a coat of arms made up of pointing fingers rampant on a blood-red field. This antagonism is terribly counterproductive and no number of management-appointed referees or high-level peace conferences will provide a solution.

Forecasting is a good example of the need for departmental cooperation. It is often looked upon as a Marketing responsibility, a task that the normal salesman detests. The salesman is uncertain as to whether to be an optimist and risk the stigma of not having met his own bogey, or be a pessimist and be held responsible for not having goods to ship to the customer. The salesman hesitates to make a commitment, knowing how likely it is to be wrong and being generally unfamiliar with how the forecast will be used.

Manufacturing usually interprets Marketing's forecasts and fills in any gaps in the information provided. The result of this second guessing is quite destructive. Generally considered an act of distrust, it further widens the gap that already may divide Marketing and Manufacturing. Instead of second guessing, joint reviews and adjustments, properly understood by both Marketing and Manufacturing, can be mutually productive.

It is quite common in some successful companies to underplan the forecast in the distant future on the theory that over-optimistic forecasts will generate unneeded inventory while problems caused by over-selling realistic or pessimistic forecasts can be handled in the short term through the use of normal activities such as weekend work, adding people to second or third shifts or subcontracting. The real demand will always be different from the forecast and it is absolutely essential for Marketing and Manufacturing to sit down together and agree to a game plan so that both know how to react.

This game plan must start with an agreement as to what Marketing is to forecast. For example, it is quite common to ask Marketing for a projection of the total market for a product followed by their best judgment of what share of this market the company could command if it had the capacity to build the products. This has the all-important function of getting agreement on whether the company's business is limited by the market or by its productive capacity. Agreement also should be reached on the unique items to be forecast specifically and those products to be forecast in groups, families, or at some level other than the top level of the bills of material. Simplifications of forecast requirements go a long way toward improving interdepartmental relations as well as leading to more accurate forecasts.

The game plan also must include an agreement as to how often forecasts will be reviewed and revised and the periods they will cover. Most companies using forecasts successfully have found it appropriate to hold periodic forecast review meetings where all departments concerned participate in mutual give and take.

Engineering can make an important contribution to better forecasting by identifying products in the process of redesign which will make them more, or less, acceptable to the customer and more, or less, expensive to manufacture.

Purchasing is another activity that must be a highly cooperative effort; it should never be considered the sole province of the Purchasing Department. Some specific problems relating to lead times are discussed in Chapter 7 but Purchasing has many interfaces with other groups that must be clearly recognized. The specifications for the material or part to be procured are identified by Engineering, the quantity and desired delivery schedule are determined by Material Control, the quality level is defined by Engineering and specified by Quality Control, a vendor's capabilities may be evaluated by Manufacturing and Engineering and the purchase contract approved by the Legal Department. Purchasing, of course, is responsible for negotiating prices, terms and conditions with suppliers they select and for exerting the necessary pressure when required to get what manufacturing needs. Regardless of the formal organization, management must bring these groups into harmonious working relationships to get the *right* materials at the *right time, quality, quantity, etc.*

Inventory levels cannot be considered anyone's sole responsibility. "You can't sell from an empty wagon" is generally quoted as Marketing's reason for favoring higher levels. However, Marketing is not entirely single-minded in pressing for more and more inventory; it never relishes the task of getting rid of out-of-date or now sub-standard products resulting from earlier excesses. Manufacturing recognizes that savings come from long runs but also sees high levels of work-in-process clog the plan and that savings are susceptible to both design and schedule changes. Engineering would like to see less inventory around when a mandatory change is at hand, but more of those items needed in new designs. Even Finance, a traditional opponent of inventory, wants reductions without additional attendant costs. So, unilateral decisions as to how much inventory is *right* and where and how it can be reduced must give way to balanced evaluations which consider the trade-offs.

Customer service levels, often considered the sole responsibility of

Marketing, are nothing but blue-sky objectives without the full participation of Manufacturing, Purchasing, Material Control, Engineering and Finance in their evaluation and achievement. There are many more shared responsibilities than unique, sole responsibilities. Teamwork, not finger-pointing, is the key.

Management Handles on Execution

Management gets what it *in*spects, not what it *ex*pects. Performance must be measured. Input/output inventory reports are important controls over the aggregate activities of Purchasing, Manufacturing, Marketing and Materials Control. Actual output rates compared to planned production levels are measures of how well Manufacturing and Material Control carry out their tasks and solve their problems. Where customer service is suitably defined and measured, it can be used to evaluate how effectively Marketing and Manufacturing execute their part of the business plan. Achievement of management's objectives for turnover of inventories (or percent of sales) is an excellent composite measure of all departments' performance in the execution of the management plan. Unfortunately,

Peerless Topman Says . . .

"Measure it if you really want to control it. Then find out who is responsible for the 'misses.' "

most of these measures do not indicate clearly which department fell down when the plan is not met.

The best measure of how well the organization is executing the plan is by the comparison of actual data with the Master Production Schedule.

This provides a *handle* on the performance of Marketing, Engineering, Manufacturing, Purchasing and Material Control in meeting their responsibilities.

The importance to top management of tracking performance of each group cannot be over-emphasized. Only in this way can the diseases be distinguished from the symptoms. Analyzing the data comparing actual to plan in the detailed formal system is the only way to pinpoint responsibility for falldowns. This closing of the loop is vitally needed for control. Few companies do it.

12

PITFALLS TO AVOID

Pitfall—Let the Expediter Rule

A medium-size chain company had successfully installed a fine system and had good people running it. When it came on-line, of course, the company had many customer orders long overdue. Telephone calls came in daily from customers needing chain urgently and the chief expediter was assigned to cope with these changes. Management was afraid that the formal system wouldn't be sensitive and responsive enough to react to these special requests so the chief expediter continued to "do his thing," usually without using the formal system or even telling it what he was doing.

What this did, of course, was to insure that the system couldn't do its thing. People trying to follow the priorities established by the formal programs were continually interrupted by Big Ed shoving some unexpected orders in ahead of what was originally scheduled. This destroyed credibility in the new programs and they limped along for many months.

Obviously the real problem here was that management didn't want to face up to real capacity limitations and the need for rescheduling all the orders in the house to develop valid delivery dates. They kept hoping that the combination of new systems and Big Ed would soon get all of their troubles off their back. Actually all it did was dig the hole deeper. The formal plan was invalid and of little help in control. Ed was putting out today's fires and fueling tomorrow's. The moral is clear. *If you want the formal system to help you, you must use it to do both the planning and the expediting.* Don't let Big Ed bypass it.

Pitfall—Ignore Real Limits

A large maker of power transmission equipment had operated for several years under good control. This followed a five-year development program to install an effective manufacturing control system during which period the management had invested significant funds in developing qualified people to run the program. Good teamwork had been established between the planners and the line manufacturing people and things seemed to be running well.

The general manager retired and was replaced by a new man from another division of the corporation. He brought along his favorite controller. About this time the corporation began to put pressure on all of its operating entities to reduce inventories. Based only on their previous experience in another division, the new top management people thought the company's inventory was far too high and issued an edict to limit purchases well below the monthly rate established by the formal plan.

The controller's edict to the purchasing agent was to hold purchased material receipts to a maximum each month approximately $40,000 below planned requirements. He was given an incentive—he got to keep his job if monthly purchased receipts did not exceed the maximum. Being a good purchasing man, he was able to control the input. Of course, the orders he held out were the ones he could get vendors to delay and so he naturally focused his attention on the expensive, high-activity materials.

In a very brief period, shortages of purchased materials made it impossible to build the products scheduled in the formal system for shipment. Inventories actually increased, customer service fell dramatically and costs went up as expediting took over to try to keep some customers happy. The general reaction of these managers was, "What good is this system? We thought it was supposed to help us."

The answer's obvious. It can't help you if you don't use it. *Either execute the formal plan as it is developed or change it.* If management really wanted to use the system to reduce inventories, they should have changed the batch quantities being made in the shop, the planned levels of safety stock, or the lead times for production operations. Their only other real choice was to drop products from the master production schedule. If this was done, the formal program then could have been helpful to them. It could have shown the danger points, focused attention on the extra costs and helped keep materials in balance. By-passing makes a deadly enemy of a faithful ally.

Pitfall—Stuff the Master Production Schedule

A large West Coast manufacturer of utility equipment had a staff of good people who, working hard over several years, developed a sound system. They had a good master schedule, a fine material requirements planning program, input/output controls of capacity and even accurate records. Their delivery performance prior to installing the system had been poor and they had had a large backlog of late orders, some very late with four missed promises to the customer.

At the general manager's insistence these overdue orders were put at the front end of the master schedule. He expressed his philosophy very clearly, "If I want 100 units per month out of this plant, I must ask for 150. There is always some falloff. If I don't ask for more I'll never get what I really want."

The *past due* column in the master schedule totalled three months' worth of orders. This generated heavy past due order totals in all plant departments where capacity or material shortages made it impossible to complete the released orders for component parts and sub-assemblies. There were actually 22 weeks of past due orders in the machine shop!

Finished units were started on schedule in most cases since the structural steel and major members were available. Shortages of machined and purchased components, however, basically due to inadequate capacity in critical machine centers and suppliers, bogged down these units all over the plant. In various stages of completion, product filled the assembly areas and overflowed into the yard and even into the street.

The message in this story is clear. *If you can't make it, don't schedule it.* When an unsound formal system launches orders which then need expediting to get the right ones completed, it is true that planning more in total may help to get more of the right things made. With good formal systems, however, this is definitely not true. A master schedule must be realistic, capable of being met. The formal system can then help identify the real shortages and focus attention on the top priority work. Any other approach is self-defeating.

In this West Coast plant the proof of this came within three months of the general manager's agreeing to develop a truthful master schedule. Output doubled (it was easy to complete the almost-finished units when the whole plant concentrated on the real shortages), backlogs of behind-schedule work dropped to a normal one-week level and shortages for the next month's units were clearly identified and few in number. Tell the system the truth so it doesn't have to lie to you.

Pitfall—Too Many Action Notices

Failure to implement yesterday's plan is today's prime reason for changing tomorrow's. With present data processing capabilities, revised plans can be generated as often as desired, even on a *real-time,* continuous basis. Executing them is something else again. Action recommendations by the thousands are proof of a system's ability to be precise, not practical. Such nervousness has many causes:

- Poorly managed master production schedule. Tinkering with this causes every change, however small, to explode through all components of every bill of materials affected. Changes should be made only for compelling reasons.

- Dynamic recalculations of batch quantities, safety stocks or lead times. The costs involved in rescheduling can far exceed the apparent benefits. In the extreme, the whole value of replanning can be forfeited if action notices are so numerous they are ignored.

- *Dribbling* engineering changes. Each change can trigger many re-scheduling notices. The use of *block* changes combining many small variations can minimize this.

- Adjusting for record errors. The system will cope with the symptoms, but the disease—too many errors—should be arrested and cured.

- Reacting to scrap and rework. Where average levels of such extra needs are meaningful, the system can plan for allowances. The unexpectedly large losses, of course, should be highlighted by action notices.

- Vendor delays. Unavoidable delivery delays will always occur. Buying capacity and scheduling detailed orders on short lead times will reduce their number for many commodities.

Constant rescheduling of orders as a result of dynamic re-evaluations of the current scene can be the goal of the system designer but will never be helpful to operating people. *Unnecessary dynamism must be suppressed.* Control requires that a sound plan be established and met, day in and day out with a minimum of replanning for unavoidable changes only.

Pitfall—Illogical and Unreasonable Reactions To a Top Management Edict

All of the divisions of a large corporation received a management edict to make substantial reductions in inventory quickly. A meeting of the division managers was called at which each was to explain in detail the actions to be taken.

One by one the managers took the podium. Most promised their best efforts to use up excesses and reduce order quantities, safety stocks and lead times. Most promised renewed efforts to eliminate slow-moving and obsolete inventories. Some proposed reducing the variety of end products being offered. All agreed management's goal was an interesting objective but few went on record believing it could and would be attained. One of the more knowledgable and experienced managers went so far as to state that presently-available techniques in his division were inadequate to the task but he promised a good "college try" nevertheless.

Last to present his case was our hero, one of the newer and more aggressive managers. He obviously had decided to forego the luxury of taking a "me too" position with his peers. With a conviction that was unbelievable, he embarked on the following line of reasoning:

- Management's authority to require immediate and substantial reductions in inventory was not to be questioned. The real question was only, "In what kind of inventory will the reduction be made?"

- Such a reduction cannot come in finished goods. Results in the past have proved that present levels are minimum for the customer service vital to the life and health of the business. Past experience also proved that current stock levels of purchased items and manufactured parts were minimum if excess stockouts and high costs, destroying profit margins, were to be avoided.

- The only remaining area for significant reduction is work-in-process, which accounts for about 30 percent of present total inventory. To meet the total inventory goal would require at least a 50 percent reduction in work-in-process. Such a sizeable reduction can be accomplished quickly only by a drastic reduction in labor input started immediately and continued over a substantial period of time. A 50 percent layoff would be announced the following Monday. He planned a weekend review with his manufacturing manager to identify the individuals involved.

Top management ended the meeting abruptly if awkwardly. They called our hero into a conference which resulted in finding more suitable applications for his talents. Needless to say, his replacement did not follow through with his proposed program.

In the year that followed, continued top management pressure did result in successful inventory reduction programs throughout the company. Middle management cannot use top management edicts as an excuse for failure to do their jobs properly. If the edict is truly impractical or is likely to cause more losses than benefits, the professional manager must make the case strong enough to get it changed—even if this requires laying his job on the line.

Pitfall—All Inventory Reductions Do Not Reduce Inventory

Inventory is an account in financial records that represents an accumulation of physical goods plus some current costs that are appropriately withheld from the current profit and loss accounting until some future period. The costs of present stocks of materials and goods are withheld from the P & L statement until the final products are marketed. Obsolete materials, of course, will never be withdrawn by active sales.

Many other costs, including all sorts of start-up costs, are often amortized over the expected life of the product, and the dollar totals of inventory also reflect these. The passage of time may well indicate that the original amortization rate was incorrect. As a result, certain costs will never leave the inventory account until the amortization plan is changed. These balances, of course, do not represent real materials.

Decisions to make drastic changes in write-off procedures can result in apparently substantial changes in inventory. The financial data may change while the phsyical materials do not. The propriety of recognizing and writing off a cost now rather than delaying it until later may be entirely valid but the effect on the numbers can be misleading. Making inventory reductions by such devices cannot have the same impact on operations and profits as making more effective and economical use of physical inventories. One is a one-time game of magic numbers; the other is continuing, solid progress. *Beware of inventory reduction programs involving bookkeeping rules.* They can give the false impression that efficiencies are being effected.

APPENDIX

PLANNING AND CONTROLLING PRIORITIES AND CAPACITIES

The Mismatch Between Customer Demand and Manufacturing

There is practically always a significant difference between the way customers order a company's products and the way the company would like to manufacture them. Customer demand is characterized by variability and variety while economic manufacturing emphasizes stability and standardization. Customers expect their suppliers to accommodate cyclic demand changes and considerable variability during the cycle on short notice. Manufacturing must deal with inflexibility of labor and material flows and the limitations of existing physical facilities. Customer demand is often quite volatile; manufacturing output is subject to considerable inertia and resistance to change.

It is possible at some cost to stabilize customer demand by simply foregoing some available business during times of peak demand. It is also possible to offer price incentives to stimulate off-peak orders. Both, in addition to lost current revenues, risk the loss of future business. Introducing flexibility into the manufacturing process increases costs related to transfers, layoffs and rehirings and demands more investment to provide manufacturing facilities with capacities to meet peak demands.

As soon as limits are set on how much profit will be sacrificed to encourage improved order patterns and on how much will be invested and spent to introduce flexibility into manufacturing, a third cost, supporting the resulting inventory, will emerge to compensate for any mismatch

137

between demand and production. All of these factors are difficult if not impossible to evaluate quantitatively. Acceptable limits can be set based on judgment only, rather than rigorous computations.

Considerable study has been given to the cost advantages of a flexible labor force and billions of dollars have been spent in the mass movement of companies and whole industries to areas where the base compensation is lower and more fluctuations are tolerated. The automotive industry frequently stabilizes order patterns by insisting that dealers place firm orders and accept delivery. In all cases, the ultimate decisions are compromises among various individuals and groups rather than economic judgments based on analysis of specific costs. Optimization of the cost factors is not easy; we doubt it is even possible.

Complete, sound formal manufacturing planning and control systems can provide many facts to help make more rational decisions in this complex situation, however. An understanding of the workings of such systems can be very helpful to top-level managers in two ways:

- knowing the kind of information they can expect to receive from well-designed systems professionally operated,

- using such systems properly to evaluate the consequences of major edicts, changes in policy, shifts in markets, etc. *before the fact,* rather than being surprised at results too late.

This Appendix is designed to help develop this understanding.

Production and inventory planning is the process of dealing with flexibility to meet the desires of the customer, the need for stability in manufacturing and the resultant inventory levels to compensate for the mismatch. The process involves performing three functions effectively:

- Developing an achievable master production schedule

- Planning and controlling priorities

- Planning and controlling capacities

The master production schedule has been discussed in detail in Chapter 6.

Planning and Controlling Priorities—Definitions

Priority Planning is the process of specifying batch quantities and their start and finish dates for all items where procurement and manufacture are involved. There must be an effective ordering system that will translate the master production schedule into requirements for the needed materials on the assumptions that:

- Planned average lead times will be dependable

- Capacity will be available when required

- Materials can be obtained in time to meet requirements

Priority Control is making the right things at the right time. It is completely dependent on maintaining a balance between master schedule requirements and output rates. *If the plant and its vendors do not produce enough in total, they will not be able to hold schedule for the right items.* This rule is immutable and links priority and capacity planning and control inextricably together.

The principles of the two priority planning systems in most frequent use, the importance of dependable lead times, the application of safety stocks and the determinations of batch quantities will all be discussed in depth in this Appendix.

Planning and Controlling Capacities—Definitions

Capacity planning is the task of determining how much output is needed from plant facilities and from suppliers. If less-than-adequate capacity is available, the problem is unmanageable. The only workable alternatives in that case are to make capacities adequate or to reduce the demands of the master schedule. The ability to manipulate lead times, an important function of priority control, is completely dependent upon having adequate capacity.

Capacity control is the comparison between planned levels and actual outputs achieved and the identification of significant variances above or below plan. Corrective action must be initiated promptly if control is to be maintained, which usually means adjusting capacity, preferable in most cases to the alternative of changing the master schedule.

Both capacity planning and control will be discussed in depth later in this Appendix.

The Relationships Between Priority and Capacity

A graphic portrayal of the relationships between priority planning and control and capacity planning and control activities is shown in Figure A1-1 which is identical to Figure 4-1, page 36. Variations of this program have appeared in various published works by George Plossl as well as in other literature in the field.

Priority planning and control activities are show in the left portion of the chart and capacity planning and control on the right. A Production Plan is developed from the business planning activities and used in Re-

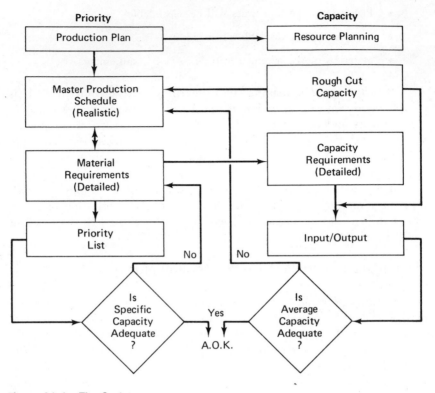

Figure A1-1   The System

source Planning for determining the necessary plant facilities and equipment. It also generates a more detailed master production schedule which, in turn, is evaluated for realism by rough-cut capacity planning approaches. The purpose of this activity is to see that the schedule does not overload the plant or fail to provide adequate work to keep the skilled people and critical equipment busy at the desired rates.

The master production schedule is translated into detailed material requirements which in turn are used to develop more detailed information on capacity requirements in specific work centers and for specific labor grades and skills. The material requirements plan provides the input to priority listings for both in-plant work and supplier's orders. This priority information is kept up-to-date as the material requirements plan is regenerated or modified.

Moving to the *capacity* side of the diagram, the rough-cut approaches or the more detailed capacity requirements determinations set the planned rates of production for critical work centers against which actual input and output of work is then compared. The diamond box on the bottom, right side of the figure contains the critical question, "Is average capacity adequate?" Here is the ultimate test of the validity of the master production schedule and the adequacy of the plant facilities and its suppliers. Emphasis at this stage of planning and control is on the word *average*. If the answer to this question is yes, a sound plan has been made and can be executed. If the answer is no, and the required capacity cannot be obtained, it is obviously necessary to revise the master production schedule to bring it into line with the capacity available.

On the *priority* side of the diagram another question is indicated: "Is specific capacity adequate?" This question arises because even sound ordering techniques release work erratically to plants and suppliers and it flows through in lumps and bunches, peaks and valleys. The amount of work to be handled by a work center will vary significantly from period to period. Ranking the work in priority sequence must be followed by an evaluation of whether or not the work center can *handle the total involved in any one period and stay on schedule.* This is another way of stating the question about specific capacity. If the answer to this question is *yes,* the plan is sound and no further action is needed. If the answer, however, is *no,* it will be necessary to revise the material requirements plan. If the overloads are large enough, even in the short term, it may even be necessary to change the master production schedule to accommodate the short-period capacity deficiencies.

The logical sequence is important. It should follow these steps:

- Develop a production plan and the necessary resource planning for long-range use

- Translate this into a master production schedule and evaluate it for realism by rough-cut capacity planning

- Develop detailed material requirements information from the master production schedule covering both released orders and planned orders to be issued in the future

- Improve the detailed planning of capacity requirements using both planned and released order information

- Develop input/output controls to insure that actual work center outputs are adequate or to highlight deficiencies so that capacity or the master schedule can be adjusted

- Develop a detailed priority list for released, purchased and manufacturing orders and keep it up to date

- Test the priorities for load implications to see if schedules will be maintained, adjusting the material requirements plan and the master production schedule if necessary

Notice that this is an iterative approach requiring frequent revisions and re-evaluations. Notice, too, it is also a closed-loop system with information feeding back on the priority and capacity interrelations. Priority and capacity cannot be controlled independently. To develop a clear comprehension of the capabilities of such an integrated system, it is necessary to understand how priority and capacity are each planned and controlled. This Appendix is intended to aid in this.

Input/Output Control

The missing link in far too many manufacturing control systems is input/output control. The report is usually set up in a format (Figure A1-2) and can be used equally well for manufacturing and purchasing. Its function is to manage lead times. It locks together priority and capacity planning.

Work Center15				All Data in Standard Hours		
			Week No.			
	27	28	29	30	31	32
Input:						
Planned	170	170	170	170	170	170
Actual	175	165	130	155		
Cum. Diff.	+5	—	−40	−55		
Output:						
Planned	200	200	200	200	170	170
Actual	205	160	180	195		
Cum. Diff.	+5	−35	−55	−60		
Work-in-process						
Planned	240	210	180	150	150	150
Actual	240	245	195	155		

Figure A1-2 Input/Output Control

This technique permits control of input rates, output rates, levels of work-in-process and average lead times. Its effective use can provide lower investment in work-in-process, better balance of production among work centers, faster response to changes in the marketplace and a more valid, stable manufacturing plan. Its introduction is recommended as soon as possible, even with very crudely set planned rates. It is the key to eliminating the Lead Time Syndrome (see Chapter 7). Capacity planning and control and priority planning and control must be linked in *both* planning and control activities. The master production schedule links the planning; input/output links control.

Planning and Controlling Priorities—The Two Basic Systems

Planning and controlling priorities for hundreds of items in dozens of work centers require a well-designed system using selected techniques capable of generating a sound plan and revising this plan as conditions change. It must react to changes in the master production schedule, reflecting changes in customer demand. It also must respond to the falldowns inevitable in a manufacturing environment. Vendors will be late, scrap will be made, machines will break down, designs and specifications will change, records will have errors—in short, Murphy's Law is always operating.

Inventory and production control systems now in use can be classed as either *order point* or *material requirements planning-based* systems. A basic understanding of the two approaches is important since their operating principles are completely different; in fact, they are opposites. Both types of systems share the same objective: to achieve good customer service at a minimum total of certain costs.

Order Point Systems

Order point approaches (called OP/OQ or ROP) attempt to have stocks of all items in continuous supply at all times. This involves choosing a stock level—the so-called 'order point'—for each item at which a replenishment order is to be placed. This stock level is selected to equal or exceed expected maximum usage during the replenishment period. Requirements for each item are usually averaged over time periods and replenishment orders are not linked to the parent items or assemblies in which they will be used.

The technique functions by comparing, as entries of issues and receipts are made, the *available* (on-hand plus already on-order) balances to the order point. Each item is handled independent of all others. As shown in Figure A1-3, no action would be taken for the part represented in weeks 1, 2 and 3 since *available* is above *order point*. In week 4, however, issuing nine units drops *available* below *order point* and triggers a replenishment order. The due date is set by adding the planned lead time. *Available* will be increased by the order quantity of 150 when the order is released for procurement or manufacture.

It is anticipated that the goal of having some material on hand at all times will be met a high percentage of the time, say 98 percent or more. It

On-Hand = 120   Order Point = 70   Safety Stock = 14   Lead Time = 4 Wks.

(Week)	1	2	3	4	5	
Forecast	14	14	14	14	14	
Actual Use	20	10	18	9		Wk
Available	100	90	72	63		8

Start 150 |◄ − − − − Lead Time − − − ► | Due 150

Figure A1-3   Order Point Technique

is recognized that the cost of attaining this goal is extra inventory called *safety* or *reserve stock.* Such systems are not capable of rescheduling those items arriving too soon when the plan is changed and this results in additional inventories. This approach is a good example of the use of inventory to attain an objective, in this case continuity of supply. For obvious reasons, such systems are frequently referred to as *stock replenishment* systems.

Material Requirements Planning Systems

Material Requirements Planning (MRP) uses an *explosion* of the master production schedule via a bill of materials to calculate the time-phased requirements for all materials, parts and subassemblies required to build the products in this master schedule.

Figure A1-4 shows a portion of a bill of materials for a pen assembly. This bill would be used in the material requirements planning technique to relate requirements for lower-level component parts to the replenishment orders for their parent items. Calculations start at the master production level (pen assembly) and cascade or explode downward to the lowest level (wire) as shown in Figure A1-5. At each level, *netting* is done for each time period by subtracting on-hand and released order balances from requirements to determine when the first new order will be needed.

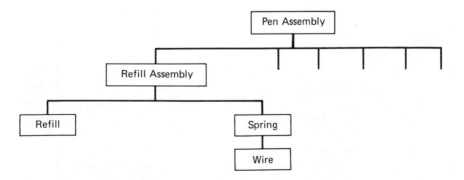

Figure A1-4   Partial Bill of Materials

Pen Assembly

Week No.	1	2	3	4	5	6	7	8
Master Production Schedule		20		30		25		35

Refill Assembly
Order Quantity = Lot for Lot   Lead Time = 1   On Hand = 10

Week No.		1	2	3	4	5	6	7	8
Required			20		30		25		35
Scheduled Receipt			10*						
Available	10	10	0	0	−30		−25		−35
Planned Due					30		25		35
Planned Release				30		25		35	

Spring
Order Quantity = Lot for Lot   Lead Time = 2   On Hand = 0

Week No.		1	2	3	4	5	6	7	8
Required				30		25		35	
Scheduled Receipt				30					
Available	0	0	0	0	0	−25		−35	
Planned Due						25		35	
Planned Release				25		35		20	

Wire
Order Quantity = 100   Lead Time = 4   On Hand = 90

Week No.		1	2	3	4	5	6	7	8
Required		10**	10	35	10	45	10	30	10
Scheduled Receipt									
Available	90	80	70	35	25	−20	−10	−30	−10
Planned Due						100			
Planned Release		100				100			

*An order for 10 now in the plant in work-in-process.
**10 per week for replacement orders from customers' spares needs.

Figure A1-5 Typical Material Requirements Planning Display

Similar calculations netting planned orders set up the whole series of planned replenishment lots in the future.

Start and completion dates for all manufacturing and purchase orders are calculated specifically and rescheduled frequently. All items are planned to arrive at their points of need at the right time and in the planned quantity. The system plans minimum levels of inventory which can include safety stocks. It needs massive data processing capability in anything but the simplest of operations.

The Evolution of the Two Systems

The oldest material control systems undoubtedly were material requirements plans. The stone-age manufacturer of war clubs must have had a master plan for production. He undoubtedly visualized a bill of material consisting of three items: one stone of certain material, shape and minimum dimensions; one stick for a handle; and some length of leather thong or sinew for attaching the stone to the stick. He could relate the number of war clubs desired to the quantity of hides from which to make thongs and of tree branches to make sticks. Production and manufacture were no doubt time-phased with schedules for matched batches of all items.

This approach continued in use into the first half of the 20th century. It was used for some extremely complex products but usually with a firm master schedule—a long backlog of customer orders. In the late 1930s it disappeared almost completely from the scene. The firm order backlogs vanished, to be replaced by variable, error-prone forecasts. The complexity of manufacture increased with more items commonly used in several end products. With processing time varying as well, the computational effort required to keep material requirements planning up-to-date exceeded the capabilities of the planning organization. It was seen that the calculating effort and the scheduling problem could be eased if continuity of material supply could be achieved and the use of order points to this end became popular, although some use had been made as early as the 1900s. The use of material requirements planning approaches was limited to massive products like ships and locomotives produced in ones and twos to firm schedules; reorder point was used for the remainder until the late 1960s.

At this time, rapidly-improving computer technology made material requirements planning again a viable technique and material control practitioners eagerly sought the advantages of a more precise, responsive and effective operating plan than reorder point could provide. Kindled by success stories and a crusade in the technical society, revived interest in material requirements planning rose dramatically and new installations proliferated.

However, all that glitters is not gold. The conversion from reorder point to material requirements planning has brought too many companies only more problems and too few, if any, real benefits. It should be approached with care and understanding, rather than with the assumption that there is only one correct technique, material requirements planning.

There is an appropriate place for both in most manufacturing operations. As Evert Welch said in an address to an APICS group, "There are no invalid techniques, just invalid applications of good techniques."

Each technique has its area of proper application. When demand for a product or an item must be forecast because it cannot be derived directly from production schedules for parent items, the reorder point technique is proper. Such demand is usually called *independent* and is based on forecasts of average usage requiring that safety stock be planned to protect against stockouts when actual demand exceeds the average.

When demand is *dependent*—meaning it is caused by schedules for packaging, finishing or assembling finished products and subassemblies or manufacturing batches of component parts from purchased or raw materials—material requirements planning is, theoretically, the proper technique. Obviously, most items of inventory have all or at least part of their demand *dependent* and properly need material requirements planning. There are, of course, exceptions to this rule, depending on commonality of parts, their value, data processing capability, completeness of bills of material and many other factors.

Which System Is Better?

The question, though frequently asked, is improper. Both techniques are needed. Material requirements planning, properly implemented, will always make the most efficient use of inventory but requires a relatively large investment in data processing. Reorder point will require more inventory but will cost less for data processing and be less precise in planning. It will require more support from informal expediting. Expensive components in a multi-tiered assembly system will almost always be best handled by material requirements planning. Inexpensive raw materials and purchased parts with wide common usage, high regularity and short lead times, can be managed economically by reorder point. There are theoretical advantages to applying material requirements planning to all dependent demand items but it seems most likely that material control in the future will continue to see reorder point used for some such items. Of course, it will be needed for items with independent demand and undoubtedly will be used in the time-phased format in most such applications.

Priority Control of Work-In-Process

The most effective control over priority is to minimize work-in-process through sound capacity planning and input/output controls, discussed in detail later in this Appendix. Without this, backlogs of work in work centers are high, lead times are long and the formal plan is extended over a long manufacturing cycle, leading to poor priority planning and frequent reschedules.

Also needed is an effective way to transmit priority information to the plant and vendors. Dates linked to material requirement planning and time-phased reorder points are frequently used. Dates on shop orders scattered through the plant are awkward if not impossible to revise; a daily priority, dispatch, or work list or a detailed schedule is preferable. Orders are ranked in priority sequence which is not rigid but from which a desirable sequence of running orders can be developed.

Such "cherry-picking" of orders out-of-sequence could be useful to combine set-ups, to use the available employee skills to best advantage, to provide urgently-needed work for downstream operations, to adapt to equipment maintenance schedules and for other such factors impossible to consider in the formal system's plan.

A requirement for sound priority control is evaluating whether or not work centers can handle the scheduled orders and keep the jobs on schedule or catch up on delays. This is the true function of machine loading. Detailed shop loading tries to determine if:

- promised delivery dates (and shop order start and due dates) can be met. This is called *loading to infinite capacity.*

- a shorter or longer delivery time is required. This is called *loading to finite capacity.*

Amateurish application of these techniques has led to some weird and wonderful results. Common among the causes of these is the belief that a remote computer can schedule a shop better than the people who live in it. Evert Welch had experience with a plant in Germany where a punch press department was always overloaded according to the load data but was constantly running short of real work. The coil-winding department, not included in the load data, was the real culprit. George Plossl has seen several plants where daily schedules developed from elegant load data were pure fiction and where there was no way to determine required or available capacity from even massive load reports.

In the very few cases where such approaches have been helpful, they have been introduced as *fine-tuning* after the basic system and its essential supports were in place and functioning and where capable people used the additional details to help them make better decisions.

Red Tags as Priority Controls

Don't overlook the effectiveness of crude tools applied at the right time and in the right way. "Red Tags" have been cursed, maligned and ridiculed but, at the proper time, they can be really helpful in identifying the capacity limitation causing priority problems. There is a right and a wrong way to use them. Hoping they'll continually solve all urgent problems is futile; firefighting is effective only when there's already a fire and where minimizing losses is the primary objective. Here's the right way to get red tags to work for real progress:

- Identify the specific units you would like to produce this week or this month.

- Out on the production floor, hang a *red tag* on each order still being worked but which is needed complete in the week or month. Don't split the order.

- Identify materials not yet in production but also needed if the final output is to be realized, find out where they are and hang red tags on each of those items or orders also.

- Specify that anyone not working on all red tags in the respective area won't be working there at all.

- Require a report to the top manufacturing person immediately when it is indicated that some red tag action cannot be completed in time.

- Limit the number of red tags to some reasonable maximum. If too many urgent actions flush out, cut back the total production target; you wouldn't make it anyhow.

- Find the bottleneck areas *and fix them.* Locate causes; don't just treat symptoms.

This simple technique with a gimmick name (the authors have called it "Country Boy," or "Red Devil") has worked quickly to highlight chronic manufacturing problems, too little capacity, engineering hold-ups, purchasing inadequacies and even a little-used electric welding machine hidden back in a corner. It is fine to say that such shortcomings shouldn't go unobserved in a well-run company but manufacturing will never live on its formal system's data processing outputs alone. An occasional exercise in utter simplicity can be helpful in an amazingly short time.

Planning and Controlling Capacities

Capacity planning is the determination of the capacities needed to achieve the desired output of the production plan, usually expressed in a master production schedule and, if actual capacities cannot be made adequate, developing suitable modifications to that schedule. When actual capacity available in the future is just equal to or only slightly more than that needed to support the formal plan, a critical capacity problem exists that is difficult to control. There are always extra unplanned demands on capacity above those of the formal plan. As the ratio of the actual capacity available to that needed becomes higher and higher, priorities are easier to control and the problem reverts to deciding which items to build into excess inventories.

The relationship of peak loads to average loads in critical areas will determine the degree to which advance scheduling must be detailed and how manufacturing lead times must be adjusted to best utilize current capabilities to satisfy future needs. The use of average lead times in material requirements planning will not be adequate to handle the priority planning to best utilize capacity.

A major function of capacity planning and control is to identify the impossible areas and to evaluate the degree of criticality of others. The objective, nearly always, is to eliminate the impossible areas by making more capacity available. Changing the master production schedule is usually the last resort. Part of the job of planning and controlling capacity is seeing that the priority planning function keeps work supplied continually to the critical areas and provides an adequate supply to less critical work centers. Input control is at least as important as output control in managing capacity.

Capacity control requires measuring whether planned capacities are, in fact, attainable and detecting and reporting significant imbalances or deviations from planned levels. *Capacity* measures thru-put rates as contrasted to *load* which measures the amount of work at a work center. Simple, rough-cut capacity plans can be very effective. The unit of measure may be as simple as sales dollars or as complex as labor or machine hours. Actual output may be defined simply as immediate past history or as *rated* or *nominal* available labor and machine hours which are calculated with great precision including appropriate allowances for machine utilization, efficiency and other factors. Capacities available in the next four to eight weeks are usually closely related to actual outputs in the last four to eight weeks. This is subject, of course, to specific changes in resources as well as to upsets such as strikes, floods, fires and so-called "acts of God." Usually it is better, however, than calculated rated levels of capacity. Like the weather, what you will get is most likely to be what you have got.

Capacity is always related to increments of time, such as operating hours per day, but large planned outputs in short increments of time can be accommodated by accumulating inputs over longer periods. For example, a work center required to produce 1,000 hours of output in any one week can be fed by one with a capacity to produce only 200 hours per week if this rate can be held during the preceding five weeks. The only valuable function of work-in-process is to decouple operations while keeping them adequately fed.

Rough-Cut Capacity Planning

Evert Welch had experience with the acquisition of a highly profitable company managed by a competent and respected individual. The plant used material requirements planning effectively back in the 1950s but the dominant and overriding consideration this manager gave to the business was his insistence that the company was a $2-million-dollar-a-month company. In this company total monthly dollar sales were quite adequate as an indication of the capacity needed to produce its output since shipments followed production immediately. He skillfully maintained a level monthly order input of $2 million to the factory by holding back excess customer orders that sometimes arrived late in the month, by coaxing old customers into add-on orders or by building some stock when the total was insufficient. At the same time, outputs were carefully monitored to the $2 million goal each month.

The new owners were accustomed to special outputs with sales drives, seasonal promotions, "president's months," and other variables, reacting to new orders received. During the time the previous owner managed the acquired company, he successfully resisted these ups and downs and maintained an orderly and profitable operation. Later, when the new owners came into full control, the surges and month-end pushes became a way of life and output and profits suffered.

When finished goods are produced well in advance of shipments to the customer or at a level rate for cyclical sales, the master production schedule is quite different from the sales forecast. Goods actually produced in past periods are then a better indicator than past actual shipments of the plant's ability to produce in the future. Many companies have substantial portions of their business in drop-shipments or nonmanufactured items. In determining capacity needs, it is necessary to segregate that part of the business not limited by in-plant capacity from that which is so limited. Where general and administrative expenses and profits vary significantly in different product lines, it is also quite likely that *cost-of-goods-sold* will be a better basis than sales. When finished goods inventories are being reduced substantially, this will not be a good indication of output needed from the factory. This reduction also must be reflected in the master production schedule and it will be lower than shipments.

In all of these relatively simplified approaches, it is assumed that the past is a suitable indicator of the plant's ability to perform in the future. And, indeed, this is very true. Capacity is a very sticky variable; it is difficult to make significant changes in short periods beyond those possible with overtime or predeveloped subcontracting.

Detailed Capacity Planning

With modern data processing facilities, it is possible to calculate in detail the required labor and machine hours using the specific release and planned order details from material requirements planning together with the shop routings, process information and work standards. Indeed, this has long been the technique of *shop loading* using Gantt charts introduced around 1900. In these earlier attempts, only released orders were loaded into work centers, Invariably, they showed immediate overloads (often called the "bow wave") from delinquent requirements in the first period, dropping off quickly to underloads later as the effect of released orders dwindled.

In more modern attempts, called *capacity requirements planning*, the explosion of master production schedules, where backlogs are not permitted, with *planned requirements* added to released orders, is supposed to give more practical results. This, however, is of questionable value in most companies. It is a massive and complex exercise in data processing, highly precise but of dubious accuracy. This results not only from errors in bills of material, routings and standards, but also because the technique ignores:

- normal backlogs needed; it assumes *all* work will be completed in the planning horizon

- new products or design changes over the horizon

- new production equipment and new or revised methods to be introduced

- significant changes in the amount of subcontracting

- unplanned requirement such as scrap, rework, record errors, etc., not in the formal plan

These must all be guesstimated and frequently represent up to 25 percent of the total demands on capacity. It makes little sense to calculate 75 percent with high precision—and at great cost—and guess the balance.

A more practical approach uses *bills of labor,* so called because of their similarity to bills of material (Figure A1-6). The standard hours cover work on *all components* of the product in the work centers listed.

These standard hours or other measures of the capacity required are extended by the numbers of units for each product family (or *typical* product or individual unit) in the master production schedule and a total capacity requirement for each important work center and vendor determined for each time period. The periods are averaged over three months or more to set planned levels of operation for each facility.

Product Family No. 12

	Work Center No.	Std. Hrs. Per 1000 Units	
Plant-	10	10	
	12	8	
	15	14	
	16	9	
	18	28	
Supplier -	Foundry	230	Molds
	Chemicals	310	Gallons
	Fasteners	4800	Pieces
	Steel	750	Pounds

Figure A1-6   Bill of Labor

This approach is admittedly approximate; it ignores lead time offsets (some centers must complete their work before others can begin), it gives no consideration to changes in inventory levels and the standard-hour data often is estimated. It is simple and very practical, however, for two important tasks:

- evaluating the master schedule for realism

- setting average planned levels of production for use in input/output controls

"Enhancements" to Reorder Point Systems

In view of the failure to recognize reality and the lack of essential supports in the form of accurate records, well-managed lead times and realistic master plans, it is surprising that reorder point techniques function as well as they do. In successful applications, order points have been determined empirically on the basis of what works and what doesn't, increasing reorder points that have been too low—indicated by excessive stockouts—and reducing those that have been too high—revealed by unused inventory. Performance also has been improved by *exploding* a master schedule into average requirements for components in the future rather than assuming that past usage would indicate future usage rates.

Assuming average usage and attempting to maintain some level of inventory at all times will require excess inventory, more than is really needed and will allow some percentage of the parts to go out of stock. These stock-outs are the source of most of the operating problems. If 10 items used in one assembly each have a 95 percent chance of being in stock, the probability that all will be available at one time to make the assembly is only 60 percent. Throw in problems from lack of the supports mentioned above, together with the usual upsets in manufacturing and it is not hard to account for the almost religious fervor of the proponents of material requirements planning to be rid of reorder points forever.

Attempts have been made to introduce supporting techniques to reduce the incidence of stock-outs with reorder point approaches. The most common of these techniques is called variously staging, pre-selection, kitting, and a variety of other names. Parts needed to assemble or process some product are checked to determine availability in advance of actual need and short lists are generated to highlight the missing parts of expediting. Such staging can be physical segregation, or paper allocating, or reservation. The principal danger in this practice is that preselection periods don't get better as they get longer. Items preselected too far in advance of use may be found to be committed to the wrong product, one which is not wanted now as urgently as some other product also using this part. The temptation is irresistible to "steal" the parts for another order, aborting the formal plan and aggravating the problem of record errors. The trick is to make the period long enough to be able to overcome shortages without being so long as to generate undesirable freezing of items or "robbing Peter to pay Paul." Its only benefit is to gain some time to overcome the basic deficiencies in an ordering technique which has been misapplied and to eliminate record errors.

A second modification to reorder point systems is an attempt to apply priority rules like *Critical Ratio* which relate *time remaining* to *work remaining* for open orders. The purpose is to overcome the system's inherent inability to keep the replenishment order due-date up to date. The idea is to recalculate periodically the priorities of a given item between the time the order is placed and the date it is due, reacting to changes in usage and/or the rate of progress of the order through the plant. If the reorder point approach is proper for the item, such applications can be useful. If the basic ordering technique is misapplied, the results are ludicrous. You can't convert the wrong technique into the right one by imposing another on it.

A very useful modification of the reorder point technique is to present the data in a material requirements planning format, using the netting logic of material requirements planning to determine when new replacement orders will be needed. Called the *time-phased reorder point*, it is illustrated in Figure A1-7 using the data from Figure A1-3. In this case, a replenishment order is needed when *available* drops below safety stock in week 8.

OH = 120		*LT = 4 Wks.*			*OQ = 150*			*SS = 14*	
Week		*1*	*2*	*3*	*4*	*5*	*6*	*7*	*8*
Required		14	14	14	14	14	14	14	14
Scheduled Receipt									
Available	120	106	92	78	64	50	36	22	8
Planned Due									150
Planned Release					150				

Figure A1-7   Time-Phased Reorder Point

This has at least three advantages:

- It permits blending the two ordering techniques into a common system where items have need for both techniques

- It looks to the future rather than waiting until the reorder point is broken to release information

- It can revise due dates on released orders

Like material requirements planning, however, it involves massive data manipulation.

"Enhancements" to Material Requirements Planning

The logic and the mechanics of material requirements planning are simple. Many enhancements have been developed, however, ostensibly to improve its usefulness. Some are beneficial but others have generated more problems than benefits. Here are the most important:

- *Dynamic order quantities*—batch quantities can now be calculated in a variety of ways. Most of these are dynamic—they recalculate lot quantities each time the material requirements planning program is run.

The harmful effects are rarely considered but frequently far outweigh the benefits. A projected requirement of 500 expected eight months in the future is certain to change many times before that month becomes reality. The cost in useless order quantity calculations is bad enough: far worse is the result of recalculated planned orders impacting fixed released orders and generating action notices to expedite or push these back. These costs are not included in the formulas; they are frequently far more than those included. Add to these tangible costs the intangible effects of unnecessary nervousness, excessive rescheduling and attention diverted from real problems. The value of such elegance is questionable.

- *Dynamic safety stocks*—discussed in more detail elsewhere in this Appendix, safety stocks when added to a material plan can often be a snare and a delusion rather than of real help. Dynamic calculations increase the odds against realizing any benefits.

- *Dynamic lead times*—this automating of the lead time syndrome discussed in Chapter 7 is to be avoided. Yet purchasing people and many in material control continue to view it as a real benefit and, worse, yet, to use it.

- *Allocations*—all components associated with a replenishment order about to be released are reserved or committed by this technique. It permits staging on paper or preselecting to test the availability of needed components and to develop, via the formal system, a shortage or expedite list in advance of release of manufacturing orders. It also helps explore alternative uses of scarce components when a number of parent items are competing for them.

- *Pegged requirements*—these identify the specific parent items which have generated requirements on any component part. This is quite useful in speeding up decisions when components cannot be made in the plant in accordance with the material plan.

- *Firm planned orders*—these act as a combination of firm orders (scheduled receipts) and planned orders not yet released. Like planned orders, the computer "explodes" them to determine the requirements on all needed components. Like firm orders, the computer does not move firm planned orders into other time periods nor does it adjust the quantity ordered. This is useful in handling special situations on lead time, order quantity or load leveling for one or a few orders without changing all future planned orders. Material requirements planning generates action notices indicating the need to expedite or delay such orders exactly as it does for firm orders already released.

Alternate Priority Control Systems

While most control systems can be classified as one or the other of the two just described there are some interesting variations found in industry.

The basic concept of reorder point most widely in use is that a relatively fixed quantity be ordered each time a replenishment order is released. This is described by technicians as a *fixed-quantity, variable-frequency* system since the time between releases of successive orders will vary as demand varies.

A variation on this theme is found where certain items are manufactured at a fixed frequency, say once a month, and the quantities are varied to meet changing usage. This is called the *fixed-frequency, variable-quantity* technique. The technique is well adapted to the maintenance of branch or warehouse stocks; here it is sometimes called sales replenishment. It is also useful in manufacturing where common tooling is used by several parts and the sequence in which they use that tooling is important. In one plant in which Evert Welch worked, some 300 parts of this type were grouped and manufactured each month, whether or not the resulting quantity of each seemed to be economical.

Generally it is handled as an *order-up-to* system. A target level is calculated to reflect requirements over the period between periodic deliveries plus some safety stock to guard against above-average demand. Each time the ordering period is reached, the quantity actually on hand plus any on order are subtracted from the target and the difference becomes the next order quantity.

When it comes to sophisticated preplanning and scheduling of shop orders, the Scandinavians have a name for it: *Cyclical Planning.* Developed by two employees of Volvo, it is used in some plants in Sweden and Norway. A key part of plan is a shop scheduling interval obtained by dividing the total work hours in a year into eight parts, called *cycles.* In turn, these *cycles* are divided into eight parts, called *periods*. This results in 64 identical time periods for planning purposes. Shopwise, the Gregorian calendar is forgotten and a schedule is specified as, "complete at *hour* 15, *period* 6, *cycle* 4."

Anyone who has tried to schedule using weeks of varying numbers of days and months of varying length can see the technical advantages of this approach. So far, there has been no acceptance of the idea in the United States but you may see some change in thinking when Volvo and other foreign industries come to this country to run plants.

The really interesting feature of *Cyclical Planning* is the development of repeating sequences for a number of manufactured parts which like to run together. Orders with a common set-up, items which use raw materials economically when run together, shading from light to dark colors and many such desirable sequences are planned to repeat each cycle. This feature alone makes study of the technique worthwhile. A cyclical plan is really a massive timetable and no claim is made by its inventors that the timetables are always met. They liken the operation of a factory without one, however, to trying to run a complex railroad on a random arrival basis—collisions would be inevitable. Whether or not you agree that the simile is appropriate, the approach has potential benefits—after you get your railroad equipment, the manufacturing control system, in good running order. Don't automate the controls until your engine can pull the full load on the right track.

Problems Common to Reorder Point and Material Requirements Planning Systems

We have pointed out the widely divergent approaches to the priority planning problem as practiced in reorder point and material requirements planning systems. Although different in approach, the end objectives of the two systems are the same—good customer service at a reasonable cost. In achieving this, there are at least three important activities that the two systems have in common, even though they use them differently.

The management of lead times is essential to both. Both find it necessary to combine successive period requirements into batches. Both find application for safety stocks. Following is an in-depth discussion of these.

Management of Lead Times

Lead time is handled by the two techniques with completely opposite methods. Both require for each item a standard lead time which represents the planned average time period between start and completion of an order. Reorder point considers these lead times unmanageable but representative of reality and lacks the facility to reschedule orders to reflect more appropriate lead times. The principal exception is new, earlier finish dates and shortened lead times on items found to be critical from preselection activities; here reorder point turns the task of getting them over to expediting.

Material requirements planning assumes the ability to manage lead times, completing work in shorter than average lead times when needed or delaying work when possible. Material requirements planning is a periodic or continual rescheduled process of changing priorities. When the longest element of lead time is waiting or queue time, this is practical. It must be recognized that foreshortened lead times for some few items getting high priority will certainly result in longer lead times for all others with lower priority. Average lead times, of course, always depend on average levels of work-in-process.

Material requirements planning hopes to gain flexibility from its data processing ability and from reaction in the plant to changing priorities. Reorder point must get it from additional inventory beyond immediate requirements.

Due Date Validity

It is a basic concept of material requirements planning that due dates on orders will be changed as necessary, usually frequently, and that operations can react to these changes. It is true, in a perfectly operating material requirements planning system, that when no eggs are delivered, no bacon will be delivered at the same time. Fortunately, there are no perfect systems. Obviously, the first requirement in getting materials on time is to know when *on time* really is and to have due dates change as needs change. Serious problems arise, however, when tinkering changes, dynamic techniques and too-frequent replanning generate more reschedules than can be handled. Such nervousness indicates poorly-managed, rather than poorly-designed systems.

Due dates also are important to reorder point for a completely different reason. Dates set at the time orders are placed are intended to bring all items to stock ahead of real need. Because actual always varies from plan, many will come in ahead, a few just in time, and some later than needed without any rescheduling. The excess inventory cost is a concommitant of the system. Which items are really going to be needed earlier or later are not known when the orders are placed and reorder point can't redefine the needs during the order cycle.

It depends on some supportive subsystems to do this. It is standard practice in reorder point systems to identify the few items that will arrive later than need by staging checks. This can fail when the number of shortages becomes excessive and occurs when people count on safety stocks and long lead times to relieve them of the need to meet due dates.

There can be no question that the material requirements planning approach to due dates is more precise. Both reorder point and material requirements planning techniques, however, simply develop a plan for replenishment. Executing the plan effectively may be more beneficial than changing it, particularly if you must live with reorder point until material requirements planning can be made available.

Management of Batch Decisions

In the days when reorder point systems prevailed, the order quantity decision seemed relatively simple. The first assumption generally made was that the item under consideration would be in continuing demand. Batches would be used up at some fairly uniform rate and any errors in the current order quantity could, therefore, be corrected on a subsequent order. The second assumption was that any component parts or raw materials would be available when needed. At the worst, the batch quantity could be corrected to match the available parts or more parts could be expedited. Demand was assumed to be in relatively small increments as compared to the order quantity.

The Economic Order Quantity was defined as the one that would minimize the sum of ordering and inventory carrying costs. Since its derivation in 1915, a formula, known variously as the Camp, Wilson, EOQ or Square Root formula, has been used to choose the quantity giving the lowest sum of these two costs.

A few theoreticians have reasoned that batch size has an effect on safety stock, realizing that the more often batches are run, the greater the frequency of exposure to a stock-out. Almost none have tried to reverse the process and adjust the batch size to reflect the costs of stock-outs. Others have modified the formula in manufacturing operations where the rate of manufacture is only slightly greater than the rate of usage. Few have considered any limitation on the total units required. A batch of 90 isn't very economic if the *forever* requirement is 100. A batch of 90 followed by one of 10 is hardly better than two orders of 50 each or one for 100.

None have considered that the initial requirement must be satisfied and, since there is no option, it should not come into the order quantity analysis. If the immediate need is to meet a withdrawal of 50, that is the minimum; the economics of the situation have to do only with how many more are required and should be run now to be carried in inventory until needed. Quantity discounts on purchased items have been brought into the picture in a variety of formulas, all of different form from the original EOQ calculation.

Since order quantity decisions had to be made and since nothing else available offered a better solution, the EOQ formula experienced a reasonable amount of application, some in situations where it was appropriate, but too often where it didn't fit well at all. If the quantity ordered was used eventually, there was little to signal the fact that a different quantity would have been more economical. If supporting quantities were not available for the chosen quantity of a parent assembly, it could be adjusted with the hopes that there would be better luck next time. Costs more significant than those in the formula were ignored and the aggregate effect of the individual decisions on capital investment, cash flow, space and capacity of machines was not apparent and often harmful. More people were hurt than helped to real savings.

One small blessing was available. Once started in the system, there was little temptation to adjust the quantity in flight, so to speak, to reflect changes since the start of the order. Quantities of 500 or 1,500 might now be better adapted to current needs than the 1,000 in-process, but the technique gave no indication of the need to change.

Material Requirements Planning Batch Decisions

Material requirements planning with its precise calculations of requirements in time periods brought with it a tremendous capacity for improving the economics, both in the ability to handle more complex formulas and in periodic or continuous recalculations. A degree of sophistication unthought of in reorder point days was possible and the technicians responded with enthusiasm producing a spate of proposed order quantity algorithms. Least total cost, least unit cost, part-period balancing, period order quantities, lot-for-lot and Wagner-Whitin's algorithm were added to the tool box.

Immediate advantage was taken of the fact that usage was projected in discrete quantities in small time *buckets* well out into the future. The fact that the first period requirement is a must and does not enter into the calculation became part of most formulas. Wagner-Whitin's complex simulation chose a combination of sequential order quantities to minimize costs but assumed that the data at hand represent a complete view of the horizon. IBM developed a formulation feature called, "Look ahead, look back," which searched the requirements sequence for large quantities to be shifted to get small improvements in the economics.

All of these approaches assumed, as did the original EOQ concept, that the best order quantity produces the lowest sum of the order and inventory costs. The opportunities for re-evaluating optimums in dynamic replanning systems are unlimited and many proponents of material requirements planning have tried to make this a real virtue. To their credit, system designers have abandoned the idea of changing an actual order quantity while it is in process. To their debit, however, must be charged the tunnel vision which focuses on one item as if it existed in a void, ignoring its links to parents and components in a bill of materials.

They overlooked essentials in the situation. When a master schedule is projected far enough into the future to provide a horizon long enough to make it useful for the ordering of long lead time materials at the lowest levels in the bills of material, the only thing certain is change.

The Use of Safety Stocks

There are three types of safety stocks used in today's manufacturing systems:

- Reorder point safety stocks

- Material requirements planning safety stocks (including time-phased reorder point)

- Special situation safety stocks

These safety stocks are significantly different and these differences should be understood. More has been written about reorder point safety stocks, including applications to the time-phased order point, than any other inventory control subject with the possible exception of the economic order quantity. Almost every published work on the general subject of safety stock is related to the reorder point problem.

Very little has been written about material requirements planning safety stocks. Most of the literature simply describes the mechanics of handling safety stock in the material requirements planning environment. Many attempts have been made to transfer reorder point methodology to material requirements planning but they have been uniformly unsuccessful. The reasons are that the operating characteristics of the two ordering techniques are diametrically opposed and the basic theory of reorder point calculations is not applicable in material requirements planning. This will be discussed in more detail later in this Appendix.

Special situation safety stocks have had a wide variety of applications and have been the subject of many case studies. The story of the "Berlin Stocks" later in this Appendix is one example.

Reorder Point Safety Stocks

In reorder point systems, every item at every level of production stands on its own. The primary objective is continuity of supply at all levels at all times. The key to success is the determination of *maximum planned usage rates* for each item. The better this can be known over the item's lead time the better it can be determined how much stock is needed on hand when a reorder is placed so that there will be continuity of supply over the replenishment period. Discontinuity does not occur while the stock on hand is being used up; it occurs when the stock on hand has been used up, so replenishment orders must be placed while there is still enough stock on hand to satisfy maximum demand over the lead time.

The reorder point, for which the technique is named, is the planned maximum usage during a replenishment lead time. There always will be some failures to determine the proper value for this planned maximum. The concept is that reorder points should be large enough for success in a high percentage of the cases, say 98 percent or 99 percent. However, since the inventory that results is directly related to the reorder point, it should be small enough to result in an occasional stockout, say one percent to two percent. Hopefully, such a stockout frequency will be acceptable, meaning preferable to carrying more inventory.

The determination of this *right* reorder point has been the subject of volumes of literature on a multitude of approaches, mostly statistical in nature. Strangely enough, very few practitioners have met the problem head on and, in applying reorder points, asked the direct question, "For what maximum demand should we plan?"

A few companies, most of them in Europe, have attempted to calculate these maximums from explosions of the master plan. In such cases, averages are usually developed first and then factored for seasonal and batching effects. Even when historic data is in extensive use, we know of no companies who have reviewed history to determine what has been experienced in maximum usages over lead times. This may have been a significant factor in explaining why reorder point systems fell so quickly into disrepute in the 1960s when faced with the cold, simple logic of material requirements planning.

The accepted method of determining a reorder point is typically the statistician's approach. The first step is to determine the expected *average* usages for future time periods which is itself a very difficult determination. Too few companies have gotten that number from a master plan; most depend upon history on the assumption that recent demand history is a good indication of future needs.

The second step is to determine the statistical pattern of the variability of demand about that average. This determination is based solely on history, and provides a real field day for the statistical fraternity. While there may be some study of real demand patterns, the usual assumption is that variability about the average will follow *normal* or *Gaussian* laws. Some adventuresome theorists have tried variations, using the *Poisson* distribution, while others have experimented with such esoteric distributions as *log normal, exponential,* and *chi-squared.*

Actual variabilities about the average are described in statistical measures, usually the *standard deviation* or the *mean absolute deviation,* on a per-period basis. This is then converted to the *standard deviation over the lead time period* on the basis of some very shaky mathematics. A *management approved service level* is substituted for *maximum planned usage* and a table is consulted giving a number of standard deviations corresponding to the service level. That number of deviations times the value of one deviation produces a calculated amount of safety stock which, when added to the average demand, provides a reorder point. These calculations are made for each item under control of the technique. Many practitioners believe better control will result if the calculations are repeated frequently, even weekly, but there is no real evidence that this is true.

This is pretty heady stuff and it might seem to have little chance to be successful. Recognize, however, that any amount of safety stock is better than none with the reorder point technique and that it is almost impossible to tell whether or not too much safety stock exists. Too little safety stock advertises itself in frequent stock-outs while too much is only obvious from a study of groups of similar items, if such, in fact, exist. It is not particularly surprising that many companies have gotten along quite well using such simple rules as, "One month of safety stock on *A* items, two on *B* and three on *C*." This does not say that these are good rules but rather that reorder point systems have a high tolerance level to unsophisticated rules.

One highly sophisticated statistical technique has enjoyed considerable application. It is called *exponential smoothing* and it performs all of the steps described above and others as well. It usually is used to make a forecast each period of the average usage for the following period for every item in the inventory. It gives more weight to recent history in making these forecasts. It observes the error of its latest forecast, averages it with past errors and does all of the computations leading to a reorder point. It then issues a report that says, in effect, "Using a complex formula, the weighted average of past usage is *x* and I suggest using this as a forecast of future average usage and for economical order quantity calculations. Using similar averages in the past, my average forecast error has been *y*, and I suggest we use that as a basis for determining safety stock."

As the frequency of planning revisions increases (with computers it can be as often as once a week) the conversion of per-period data to longer lead times becomes more and more questionable. Extrapolating one-week averages and variabilities into lead times of 12 weeks or more is at best an approximation.

All of these statistical calculations are simply a substitute for determining maximum planned usage during a lead time. It is quite easy to overlook the fact that a better answer may come from analysis of the sales plan, the manufacturing plan and capacity limitations. Manufacturing 1,000 units of some product each month sets practical limitations on monthly component parts requirements unrelated to variations of usage around some average. Service level objectives change from 98 percent of a mythical statistical potential to 100 percent of a logical maximum plan. A well-disciplined system operating within such limits will fill a high percentage of all demands without rescheduling or massive data processing to monitor period-by-period usage and react to numerous changes.

Even poorly-designed and operated systems can develop reasonable service levels from the sheer weight of excessive inventories of overadequate safety stocks. Reorder point is inventory oriented but the continuing objective must be to approach the *right* inventory level—that amount of inventory which minimizes the excess without increasing the percentage of failures.

Summarizing, the basic elements of a reorder point system are:

- an objective to accommodate planned maximum variability of demand at the top level through continuity of availability of finished products through the use of safety stock inventory

- support of the objective at all lower levels by similar continuity of availability of all components through the use of safety stocks

- no planned rescheduling or expediting action on other than a small percentage of the items where stock-outs must be cleared on an emergency basis

Material Requirements Planning Safety Stocks

To compare material requirements planning safety stocks with reorder point safety stocks, it is first necessary to understand what makes the two systems so different. Reorder point attempts to operate as if lead times could not be managed. It uses inventory in the form of safety stock to accommodate deviations from the average plan. It resists the idea of rescheduling an order while it is in process and it does all planning of lower-level items to get continuity of supply by techniques similar to those used on the top-level items.

Material requirements planning, on the other hand, operates on the theory that lead times are manageable and that they can be drastically reduced from planned lengths in the course of normal operations. It has the ability to identify the items needing reschedules and the new orders that will make the system work without relying on inventory to handle unplanned needs. It resists the idea of using safety stock as a buffer and it will propose reschedules as if safety stocks were not there. Planning of lower-level items is directly linked to those at the time level and the system will ignore safety stocks introduced at lower levels.

System modifications like pre-selections and Critical Ratio have been introduced to try to move reorder point toward a rescheduling mode. System modifications like the firm planned order have been introduced into material requirements planning to try to force it to take advantage of added inventories. None of these modifications are truly compatible and the basic system tends to reject the intrusions like the body does an organ transplant.

When you consider the problem of material requirements planning and safety stocks, you have to start by asking why the system won't operate without them. Lower-level items are linked to the master production schedule and are replanned on a period-by-period basis. The logic is straightforward but the thousands of items that may be covered by the material requirements planning program require massive data processing facilities. No matter what supports are introduced at these lower levels (such as safety stock) the system will try to reschedule all of these lower-level items as top-level schedules change.

Because safety stocks at these lower levels seem to serve no useful purpose, material requirements planning practitioners are in general agreement they are likely to be more trouble than they are worth. The one exception to this rule is at the bottom level of bills of material—raw materials and purchased parts from vendors. Late deliveries from suppliers are common and their lead times are not nearly as manageable as those within a company's own operations so it becomes general practice to schedule vendor shipments one or more periods in advance of expected need. There are strong arguments in many businesses that favor staying with reorder point at this level and seeking continuity of supply by using safety stocks. There seem to be equally strong reasons to use no safety stocks at intermediate levels. A good question arises as to whether or not there is real application for safety stocks at the top level of bills of material.

If there is, it seems most likely that it will occur in those items designated as having *independent demand,* such as spare parts, base units and optional equipment or accessories. In these cases, the most appropriate forecast seems to be for some average usage per planning period with an extra potential requirement over some period, say a lead time. A typical situation would be an average demand of 100 per planning period with the possibility of needing an extra 200 in the course of a four-period lead time.

This is exactly the situation to which reorder point is so well adapted—a *planned maximum usage per lead time* of 600, interpreted as an average of 100 per planning period and a safety stock of 200, to be adjusted for actual requirements as time passes. Using reorder point for these particular items might be attractive, but its methodology isn't compatible with material requirements planning. Practitioners have developed a solution that they call time-phased order point discussed earlier in this Appendix. *Time-phased* indicates the adaption to material requirements planning format and logic; *order point* recognizes that they are dealing with averages and maximums. There is a strong tendency to assume that this has to mean the use of safety stocks whether or not they are appropriate to the problem. In fact, many efforts have been made to use the same safety stock that would have been used in the earlier system, and to extend the use of safety stocks to the lower levels.

In the final analysis, at any level and without regard to the size of the safety stock, material requirements planning will produce all of the rescheduling action notices that it would take to manage the variability without safety stock. If the attempted management of lead times fails and some safety stock is used to meet a requirement, the material requirements planning system will take every step to see that it is re-established as soon as possible, not because it is needed but just because it is there. When period usages have substantial variances around their average values, it is quite possible to have a rescheduling action every planning period for each top-level and most supporting items. Well-managed master schedules may be more stable, but uncertainty is the name of the game there, too.

It is a well-established fact that highly responsive and rigorous material requirements planning programs will reschedule items every review period to reflect any change in plan. *Such nervousness or jitters cannot be eliminated by planning safety stock; Material Requirements Planning will not use the stock available as a buffer; it protects it by rescheduling.* Material requirements planning and safety stocks are simply incompatible. The best approach seems to be to plan all items, other than purchased materials, without any safety stock and let the system track real due dates. Then react quickly to take care of unexpected problems. Any attempt to make a direct transfer of order point safety stock techniques to material requirements planning is doomed to failure.

It must be recognized that the ability to provide safety stocks in reorder point and the ability to reschedule and react quickly and effectively in material requirements planning both depend on having adequate capacity available. Most of the problems of implementing material requirements planning recommendations are ultimately capacity problems and most of the stock-outs with reorder points are not the fault of the ordering formula but rather result from the lack of capacity to meet the plan. No mathematical manipulation of numbers will provide capacity where it doesn't exist. Where capacity is borderline and allocation on an item-by-item basis is necessary, a serious scheduling problem exists and will require disproportionate attention from the best people using a rigorous material requirements planning approach even when material requirements planning programs are not the formal planning device.

It is true that most items can be produced in normal batch quantities in a matter of a few hours rather than the weeks or months of lead time normally planned. This requires high priorities and the availability of capacities that may have to be usurped from other items. *Capacity must be provided for both planned and unplanned requirements.* The idea of planning *safety capacity* is an alternative to safety stock in material requirements planning systems is getting a lot of attention in the field.

Special Situation Safety Stocks

People have envisioned many unique needs and provided for all sorts of special situations. Generally, these safety stocks are physically isolated and are to be used only under very specific circumstances. More often than not, they are a one-shot, short-term thing and are rarely built into a control system as regularly-used tools. For example, it is quite common to anticipate the possibility that a supplier company or an industry is going on strike. Many companies have built up stocks of steel as industry contract negotiations approach and have consumed those stocks after a settlement is reached. For several years, the semi-conductor industry experienced high scrap and rework rates. It was quite common for both the vendor and the customer to accumulate safety stocks to absorb the unexpected scrap and delays.

One special case is of interest. We are all familiar with the Berlin blockade and airlift and it is easy to understand the consequences to industry. Built up after the fact and never used, it is still a good example of a special situation safety stock.

The "Berlin Stock Story"

The simplest form of safety stock was the "Berlin Stock" created in that city after its historic blockade by the Russians. The blockade all but paralyzed the city and would have done so completely had it not been for the massive airlift put into action by the United States and allied nations. This airlift brought in enough vital supplies of food, fuel and medicine to keep the city alive over the critical period. But it was still impractical to airlift heavy raw materials and other commodities in enough volume to keep industry going and so industry came to an early halt.

When the blockade was over, the city government was determined to avoid a repetition of this misfortune. All manufacturers were asked to list such raw materials and other imported items as would guarantee a continuous manufacturing load for three months. These materials were ordered and financed by the city and stored in special warehouses. This was the "Berlin Stock."

To those companies involved, the term "Berlin Stock" has come to be a generic term meaning a special safety stock of materials with a long procurement period, a low probability of need but of major impact on operations if the need occurs. Every manufacturer has some need for "Berlin Stocks." The items chosen and the amounts held are generally matters of judgment rather than rigorous calculations involving the costs of inventory and the consequences of stockouts.

How Are Safety Stocks Created?

Safety stock is created when the first order is received by designating an appropriate quantity of that order as safety stock. In reorder point, there is no further consideration of the problem except that the next replenishment order is dated as if the safety stock did not exist. Incursions into the safety stock are ignored and have no effect on subsequent orders.

In material requirements planning, the following replenishment order is also dated as if the safety stock did not exist, as are all of the dependent lower-level requirements. As the top-level stock is reduced to the safety stock level, or below, the material requirements planning system goes through all of the emergency proposals that it would if the safety stock did not exist. No matter how long the safety stock might be designed to last and no matter how much is used to provide good customer service, the system will attempt immediate re-establishment of the stock. When the replenishment order does arrive, the safety stock is designated and, in effect, set aside.

In Summary

Safety stocks should not be carried as a panacea. There should be clearly defined reasons for their existence. If planned for a particular contingency, their use should be limited to meeting that contingency. Safety stock in reorder point is there to insure meeting maximum demands, using inventory in place of mass data processing. The presence of safety stock in the material requirements planning environment distorts the very information material requirements planning is supposed to furnish, valid start and due dates from orders. Safety stock in material requirements planning is justified only to whatever extent anticipated variations cannot be managed through the use of material requirements planning's inherent ability to react quickly to change and to describe the necessary corrective actions.

BIBLIOGRAPHY

Bittel, Lester R., *Management By Exception*, McGraw-Hill Book Company, New York, 1964.

Drucker, Peter F., *Management Tasks, Responsibilities, Practices*, Harper & Row, New York, 1973.

Mann, Roland (Ed.), *The Arts Of Top Management: A McKinsey Anthology*, McGraw-Hill Book Company, New York, 1971.

Martin, J. and Norman, A. R. D., *The Computerized Society*, Prentice-Hall, Inc., Englewood Cliffs, New Jersey, 1970.

Mather, H. F. and Plossl, G. W., *The Master Production Schedule*, 2nd Edition, Mather & Plossl, Inc., Atlanta, Georgia, 1977.

Plossl, G. W., *Manufacturing Control: The Last Frontier For Profits*, Reston Publishing Company, Reston, Virginia, 1973.

Plossl, G. W. and Wight, O. W., *Production And Inventory Control*, Prentice-Hall, Inc., Englewood Cliffs, New Jersey, 1967.

Townsend, Robert, *Up The Organization*, Alfred A. Knopf, New York, 1970.

Welch, W. E., *Tested Scientific Inventory Control*, Management Publishing Corporation, Greenwich, Connecticut, 1956. (out of print)

INDEX